D1126212

The British
Monarchy

Andrew A. Kling

FREE PUBLIC LIBRARY, SUMMIT, N.J.

LUCENT BOOKS
A part of Gale, Cengage Learning

GALE
CENGAGE Learning·

Detroit • New York • San Francisco • New Haven, Conn • Waterville, Maine • London

© 2012 Gale, Cengage Learning

ALL RIGHTS RESERVED. No part of this work covered by the copyright herein may be reproduced, transmitted, stored, or used in any form or by any means graphic, electronic, or mechanical, including but not limited to photocopying, recording, scanning, digitizing, taping, Web distribution, information networks, or information storage and retrieval systems, except as permitted under Section 107 or 108 of the 1976 United States Copyright Act, without the prior written permission of the publisher.

Every effort has been made to trace the owners of copyrighted material.

LIBRARY OF CONGRESS CATALOGING-IN-PUBLICATION DATA

Kling, Andrew A., 1961-
  The British monarchy / by Andrew A. Kling.
    p. cm. -- (World history)
  Includes bibliographical references and index.
  ISBN 978-1-4205-0790-4 (hardcover)
  1. Great Britain--Kings and rulers--Juvenile literature. 2. Queens--Great Britain--Juvenile literature. 3. Great Britain--Kings and rulers--Biography--Juvenile literature. 4. Queens--Great Britain--Biography--Juvenile literature. 5. Monarchy--Great Britain--History--Juvenile literature. 6. Great Britain--Politics and government--Juvenile literature.
  I. Title.
  DA28.1.K58 2012
  941.009'9--dc23

                                                    2012021861

Lucent Books
27500 Drake Rd.
Farmington Hills, MI 48331

ISBN-13: 978-1-4205-0790-4
ISBN-10: 1-4205-0790-7

Printed in the United States of America
1 2 3 4 5 6 7 16 15 14 13 12

3 9547 00388 6988

Contents

Foreword

Each year, on the first day of school, nearly every history teacher faces the task of explaining why his or her students should study history. Many reasons have been given. One is that lessons exist in the past from which contemporary society can benefit and learn. Another is that exploration of the past allows us to see the origins of our customs, ideas, and institutions. Concepts such as democracy, ethnic conflict, or even things as trivial as fashion or mores, have historical roots.

Reasons such as these impress few students, however. If anything, these explanations seem remote and dull to young minds. Yet history is anything but dull. And therein lies what is perhaps the most compelling reason for studying history: History is filled with great stories. The classic themes of literature and drama—love and sacrifice, hatred and revenge, injustice and betrayal, adversity and overcoming adversity—fill the pages of history books, feeding the imagination as well as any of the great works of fiction do.

The story of the Children's Crusade, for example, is one of the most tragic in history. In 1212 Crusader fever hit Europe. A call went out from the pope that all good Christians should journey to Jerusalem to drive out the hated Muslims and return the city to Christian control. Heeding the call, thousands of children made the journey. Parents bravely allowed many children to go, and entire communities were inspired by the faith of these small Crusaders. Unfortunately, many boarded ships were captained by slave traders, who enthusiastically sold the children into slavery as soon as they arrived at their destination. Thousands died from disease, exposure, and starvation on the long march across Europe to the Mediterranean Sea. Others perished at sea.

Another story, from a modern and more familiar place, offers a soul-wrenching view of personal humiliation but also the ability to rise above it. Hatsuye Egami was one of 110,000 Japanese Americans sent to internment camps during World War II. "Since yesterday we Japanese have ceased to be human beings," he wrote in his diary. "We are numbers. We are no longer Egamis, but the number 23324. A tag with that number is on every trunk, suitcase and bag. Tags, also, on our breasts." Despite such dehumanizing treatment, most internees worked hard to control their bitterness. They created workable communities inside the camps and demonstrated again and again their loyalty as Americans.

These are but two of the many stories from history that can be found in the pages of the Lucent Books World History series. All World History titles rely on sound research and verifiable evidence, and all give students a clear sense of time, place, and chronology through maps and timelines as well as text.

All titles include a wide range of authoritative perspectives that demonstrate the complexity of historical interpretation and sharpen the reader's critical thinking skills. Formally documented quotations and annotated bibliographies enable students to locate and evaluate sources, often instantaneously via the Internet, and serve as valuable tools for further research and debate.

Finally, Lucent's World History titles present rousing good stories, featuring vivid primary source quotations drawn from unique, sometimes obscure sources such as diaries, public records, and contemporary chronicles. In this way, the voices of participants and witnesses as well as important biographers and historians bring the study of history to life. As we are caught up in the lives of others, we are reminded that we too are characters in the ongoing human saga, and we are better prepared for our own roles.

Important Dates at the Time

1215
England's King John signs Magna Carta at Runnymede.

1325
Tenochtitlán, capital city of the Aztec Empire, founded (site of modern Mexico City).

1619
First African slaves taken to British North American colonies at Jamestown.

1492
Christopher Columbus makes his first voyage to the Americas.

1152
Temple of Angkor Wat completed in what is now Cambodia.

800	1000	1200	1400	1600

1275
Marco Polo reaches Kublai Khan's summer palace at Shangdu.

1644
Manchu invaders overthrow China's Ming dynasty and establish the Qing dynasty.

1066
Norman leader William the Conqueror becomes king of England.

1455–1485
Period of intermittent civil war in England now called The Wars of the Roses.

1558–1603
Reign of England's Queen Elizabeth I.

of the British Monarchy

1649
England's King Charles I defeated by parliamentarian forces and executed, leading to the Commonwealth period.

1936
England's King Edward VIII abdicates throne; succeeded by his younger brother, who becomes King George VI.

1837–1901
Reign of England's Queen Victoria.

1969
U.S. astronauts of *Apollo 11* make first manned moon landing.

1650 — **1750** — **1850** — **1950** — **2050**

1776
Thirteen North American British colonies declare independence from the British Empire.

1914–1918
World War I

1939–1945
World War II

2011
William, Duke of Cambridge, second in line to the British throne, marries Catherine "Kate" Middleton.

1810
Hawaiian Islands united under King Kamehameha I.

1997
Death of Diana, Princess of Wales, in auto accident in Paris, France.

1952
England's Queen Elizabeth II ascends the throne.

Introduction

A Royal Wedding

On April 29, 2011, billions of people around the world turned their attention to London, the capital city of the United Kingdom of Great Britain and Northern Ireland. The day's events were preceded by months of preparation and anticipation and culminated in the wedding of His Royal Highness Prince William Arthur Philip Louis and Catherine Elizabeth Middleton in London's regal Westminster Abbey.

At the time of the wedding, Prince William, less than two months shy of his twenty-ninth birthday, was second in line to the throne of Great Britain, behind his grandmother, Queen Elizabeth II, and his father, Charles, the Prince of Wales. Catherine, better known as Kate, had turned twenty-nine the previous January and is the first of three children born to Michael and Carole Middleton, who made their fortune in the mail-order business. William and Kate first met at the University of St. Andrews in Scotland in 2005, where she was majoring in art history. He was majoring in geography, with the anticipation of pursuing a career in the British military, as had many royal princes before him, including his father and grandfather. Kate had come to William's attention during a charity fashion show, in which she was one of the models. According to one story, William turned to a friend as Kate came down the runway and said, "Kate's hot."[1]

Their growing relationship over the next several years was the subject of gossip, rumor, and speculation, as they were seen together at events and on skiing vacations. During that time, Kate was exposed to the intense media attention and scrutiny that comes with being connected to the British royal family. Observers wondered whether William would propose to her and—as time passed—what was taking him so long to do so. When they announced their engagement in November 2010, William explained that he had wanted to give Kate time to be sure that she was ready and willing to endure the pressure of being his wife and, perhaps, someday being queen of Great Britain. He said, "I wanted to give her a chance to see in and back out if she needed to before it all got too much."[2] When he proposed, William offered Kate the same ring worn by his late mother, Diana, Princess of Wales.

Billions of people around the world watched the televised wedding of British royal couple William and Kate (center) on April 29, 2011.

From the start, the couple was intimately connected with the plans for the wedding. Mixing the modern with the traditional, they opted for a ceremony at Westminster Abbey that featured live trees that would later be replanted. The members of the wedding rode to the abbey in limousines but left in horse-drawn royal carriages, giving the 1.5 million people in attendance a chance to see the newlyweds and their families. In addition, the events were carried on live television and streaming Internet to billions of viewers around the world.

The day returned the British monarchy to the attention of people in Great Britain and around the world. A *monarchy* (meaning "one ruler") is a system of government based on heredity, in which the sole ruler, a king or a queen, passes the reins of power to his or her children. This system of inheritance places priority on the eldest child, and traditionally, in most cases, the eldest male child, who is assumed to be the heir to the throne, or the successor to the current monarch. At the time of William and Kate's wedding, William's father Charles was the heir to the throne. Charles's title, the Prince of Wales, is traditionally conferred on the monarch's eldest son, who is the heir to the throne. If Charles becomes king, then his eldest son, William, will become the Prince of Wales, and Kate will become the Princess of Wales.

A monarchy also features an abundance of titles, such as prince, princess, duke, duchess, earl, and countess. These titles designate not only the line of succession but the intimate connections to the ruling family. Many are passed down from generation to generation, while others are conferred upon the recipients by the monarch by proclamation. In a royal society, they bring enhanced prestige and recognition. British history is filled with stories of individuals who were not members of the royal family but received titles for military or political accomplishments. In other cases, the monarch adds a title to a relative in order to clarify family roles. For example, when William and Kate became engaged, there was a great deal of speculation about Kate's new formal title. On the day of their wedding, Queen Elizabeth II conferred the title of Duke of Cambridge upon her grandson, which instantly made Kate the Duchess of Cambridge.

The ability to change lives and fortunes is a hallmark of the long history of the British monarchy. The lure of its power and prestige was the focus of generations of backroom and bedroom politics and international intrigue. Its history includes wars between nations, between fathers and sons, and between brothers, cousins, and rank outsiders. Over the centuries, the role of the kings and queens of the dominion has changed with the times—sometimes peacefully, sometimes violently—but the British monarchy's ability to adapt to an evolving society marks it as one of the most successful on Earth. And while modern Great Britain now encompasses England, Scotland, and Wales, in union with Northern Ireland as the United Kingdom, the current monarchy has its origins in the ancient rulers of England.

Chapter One

Medieval England

In the year A.D. 871 a man named Alfred was declared king of Wessex, a kingdom in the south of the island of Britain. He had led successful military campaigns against Viking raiders, and in the following years helped defeat further invasions before negotiating a peace treaty with his enemies in 878 that lasted until 893. The neighboring kingdoms of East Anglia and Mercia were invaded by the Danish Vikings yet again, but Alfred's strong fortifications kept them out of Wessex.

Today Alfred is known as "the Great," not only for his success against the Viking invaders, but also for his efficient management of his lands, maintaining peace with his neighbors, and initiating a widespread campaign of education. Alfred married the daughter of a Mercian nobleman, and Alfred's grandson, Athelstan, ruled from 924 to 929. Athelstan united Wessex and Mercia against the Danes, who ruled in East Anglia. He declared himself "King of the English," and his descendants brought the kingdoms of East Anglia and Northumbria in eastern and northern England, respectively, under their rule as well. At the same time, Viking raiders had conquered a territory in the north of modern France, which they called Normandy (from the word "northman" in Scandinavian).

By the middle of the eleventh century, the kings of England had firm control over the southern part of the island. England's king, Edward, was the son of King Ethelred the Unready (Alfred's great-great-grandson) and his second wife, Emma. She was the daughter of Robert I, Count of Normandy. Edward, therefore, was half Norman, and in fact had spent much of his youth in Normandy. He was known as "The Confessor" for his deep religious convictions and was committed to Christianity and to expanding the church's presence in his kingdom. But Edward had no children,

Alfred the Great was declared King of Wessex in 871. He is considered England's first king.

and as he grew older, two men, Harold Godwinson, Earl of Wessex, and William, Duke of Normandy, began to lay plans for claiming the crown of England for themselves when Edward died.

The Year of Three Kings

Matters came to a head when Edward died in January 1066. The most powerful families in England gave their allegiance to Harold, and he was crowned king of England almost immediately after Edward's death. Harold had been one of Edward's most effective administrators and his most powerful military leader, and many had considered him Edward's

heir to the throne. But at the same time, in Normandy William prepared to claim the throne for himself.

William's claim to the throne of England was not just based on a desire for power. According to William, when he had visited Edward in 1065, the aging king assured William that he would be king when Edward died. Like Edward, William was also related to Ethelred and Emma; William's grandfather was Emma's brother. This made William and Edward cousins. William, however, was known as "The Bastard," as he was the illegitimate son of Robert the Magnificent, Duke of Normandy. When

Robert died in 1035, William was only seven or eight years old. He inherited his father's lands, and by the time he reached his early thirties he was a battle-tested leader who had defeated many of his regional rivals. William was incensed when Harold was proclaimed king but he bided his time. He wanted the throne, but he also wanted to be as prepared as possible for when he thought the time was right to claim the English throne.

Finally, William assembled an army and a fleet of ships to invade England. In October 1066, he landed on England's

The *Domesday Book*

On Christmas Day 1085 William the Conqueror resolved to send commissioners of inquiry throughout England to learn all they could about the kingdom. They were instructed to find out who held the land, who lived on the land, what property existed on it, how much it was worth, and perhaps most importantly, how much revenue it generated. The commissioners did a thorough job. According to the *Anglo-Saxon Chronicle*, an invaluable record of the time, "So very narrowly, indeed, did he commission them to trace it out, that there was not one . . . yard of land, nay . . . not even an ox, nor a cow, nor a swine was there left, that was not set down in his writ."

William's "great inquest" involved an estimated ten thousand people and covered 13,418 places, but did not survey the major towns of London and Winchester. The results were presented to him in September 1086. In the centuries that passed, the survey became known as the *Domesday Book* (pronounced "doomsday") because its written record was considered the official record of the kingdom and was not subject to appeal, as in the fate of mankind during the Christian Judgment Day.

The Online Medieval and Classical Library. *The Anglo-Saxon Chronicle*, Part 6: A.D. 1070–1101. http://omacl .org/Anglo/part6.html.

In order to learn more about his new kingdom of England, William the Conqueror commissioned the Domesday Book.

south coast to little opposition. Harold was in northern England, fighting a Viking incursion, when he learned of William's landing. After defeating the Norse intruders, he led his army to the south coast where William was lying in wait. After a long day of fighting at the Battle of Hastings on October 14, Harold and his brothers were killed on the battlefield and his remaining army fled.

The victorious William and his army made a long and circuitous trek to London, defeating resistance along the way before he claimed the throne. He was crowned king of England on Christmas Day 1066. Since that time, 1066 has been called "the year of three kings," and William of Normandy became known as William the Conqueror.

Norman Rule

During William's years as king of England (reigned 1066–1087), he solidified his hold on the land while simultaneously ruling Normandy. He defeated a series of English revolts and granted territories confiscated from defeated nobles to Norman barons who had supported his claim. He had several hundred wooden castles built across England to protect his allies against further rebellious attacks. He imposed the Norman language and political practices on the kingdom. He commissioned the creation of the Bayeux Tapestry, which depicts his invasion of England and victory at Hastings, and which survives to this day.

William's will designated his oldest son, Robert, as Duke of Normandy, granting him rule over the French part of his dominion. His youngest son, Henry, was expected to join the church and was therefore given a good education. William also imported a European tradition into England when he designated an heir to the throne: his second son, also named William.

Upon his father's death in 1087, the new king, who called himself William II (reigned 1087–1100), was eager to keep a firm hold on England, but support among many of his father's allies was uncertain. For helping the Conqueror's cause, they had received territories in England while also owning lands in Normandy. They faced a dilemma summed up by the new king's uncle, Odo of Bayeux: "How can we give proper service to two mutually hostile and distant lords? If we serve Duke Robert well we shall offend his brother William, and he will deprive us of our revenues and honors in England. On the other hand if we obey King William, Duke Robert will deprive us of our patrimonies [inheritances] in Normandy."[3]

Relations between William and his brother Robert were never cordial, and when Odo and other Norman barons in England rebelled against William, Robert stayed in France and did not offer assistance. William fought off the challenge and defeated the rebels. He also reached accords with Scots leaders to the north and Welsh leaders to the west to help keep the peace.

William II enjoyed food, drink, and entertainment. When he died in a hunting accident in 1100, some contemporary observers believed that his younger brother Henry, who was also hunting in the vicinity, had arranged the king's death, because it was Henry, not his older brother Robert, who seized the throne. William II left behind a legacy as a skilled campaigner and an effective administrator, but his brother Henry surpassed both William and their father in consolidating Norman rule in England during the next thirty-five years.

Henry I (reigned 1100–1135)

In 1098, two years before William II's death, Duke Robert had turned over the rule of Normandy to William when he (Robert) had joined the First Crusade, which was the first of many large military expeditions organized by the church in an attempt to win back Jerusalem and the Holy Land from the Muslims who lived there. Following William's death, news reached England that Robert was returning from the Crusade. A hastily convened council of the leading barons chose Henry as William's successor, in part because Robert had been an ineffective ruler of Normandy. After Robert's bid to win power from Henry failed, the brothers agreed that Henry would pay Robert an annuity and could remain king of England for his lifetime, to be succeeded by Robert. According to

King Henry I married the king of Scotland's daughter Matilda in 1102. She proved an effective administrator in Henry's absence.

historian Mike Ashley, "In the eyes of Henry and the barons possession was nine-tenths of the law and Robert was the loser."[4] A few years later, Henry captured Robert and had him imprisoned in England for the rest of Robert's life.

Henry I secured his place on the throne by fostering good relations with the church. The support of the Catholic Church was essential as its power rivaled if not surpassed that of Europe's monarchs. A message of approval or disapproval from the pope in Rome could (and usually did) dictate who became and stayed king. Henry also made an important political alliance when he married Matilda, the daughter of King Malcolm III of Scotland. Theirs was a successful marriage, as Matilda proved an effective administrator over England during Henry's frequent sojourns in France to deal with Norman affairs. They had two daughters and two sons, and Henry cemented strong bonds with European ruling families by negotiating political marriages for the two eldest children.

Although Henry's military and political successes had placed him in a secure position by 1120, tragedy struck when his two eldest legitimate sons, named William and Richard, died when a vessel called the *White Ship* on which they were passengers sank shortly after leaving Normandy for England. Henry had chosen William as his heir; now, he only had illegitimate sons as male offspring (he had at least twenty-five illegitimate children during his lifetime). Faced with this challenge, Henry desig-

nated his daughter Matilda as his heir, but the English barons were resistant to the idea of being ruled by a woman. An additional stumbling block was that Matilda was married to Geoffrey, Count of Anjou, whose nickname was Plantagenet because he liked to wear a sprig of the common broom plant (whose Latin name was *planta genista*) in his cap. His French domain of Anjou was often at war with Normandy; the barons did not like the idea of Geoffrey Plantagenet becoming their king.

Henry I died in 1135, having kept the peace in England for thirty years. He had left no heir about whom the country could agree on as their king. As neither Matilda nor Geoffrey moved to take the throne, Henry's nephew Stephen jumped in and seized the crown.

Stephen Versus Matilda and Robert

Count Stephen of Boulogne was the son of William the Conqueror's daughter Adela and had been Henry I's favorite nephew. Upon his uncle's death, Stephen hastened from Boulogne to London. He gained the support of the people of the capital and was crowned within three weeks of Henry I's death. The speed of these events took the barons by surprise, and eventually they recognized Stephen as king of England and Duke of Normandy.

Stephen's rule (1135–1154) was secure for about three years. He was popular with the people and was a firm but fair ruler. The contemporary chronicler Geoffrey of Monmouth wrote that "by

Henry II and Thomas Becket

Henry II's powerful personality brought him into conflict with a wide range of people whom he believed prevented him from getting his way. One such conflict was with Thomas Becket, who had been Henry's personal friend for many years and his chancellor. In 1161 Henry surprised many in England when he appointed Becket to the post of archbishop of Canterbury, a leading position in the church. But none were as surprised as Henry by Becket's subsequent behavior.

The two argued over several issues, such as whether churchmen who had committed crimes should be subject to civil law. Becket became an ultrareligious cleric, championing the views of the people against the state; his disputes with Henry drove Becket into exile in France for six years. When Becket returned to England in 1170, he was hailed by the people as someone who had stood up to the king. Henry was incensed and at one point raged, "Will no one rid me of this turbulent priest?" Four of his knights took him literally, and they murdered Becket in Canterbury Cathedral on December 29, 1170.

Their actions shocked England. Henry denied ordering the murder but apologized for his knights and was pardoned by the pope. Becket was made a saint of the church in 1173.

Quoted in Antonia Fraser, ed. *The Lives of the Kings and Queens of England.* Berkeley and Los Angeles: University of California Press, 1999, p. 52.

his good nature and by the way he jested and enjoyed himself even in the company of his inferiors, Stephen earned an affection that can hardly be imagined."[5] But in 1139 Matilda and her half brother, Robert, Duke of Gloucester, began to rebel against Stephen. Matilda and Robert invaded England from France, leading to civil warfare and Stephen's capture and imprisonment in February 1141. Matilda secured the support of the leading barons and the influential bishop of Winchester, and she was proclaimed "Lady of the English." Although she was never crowned queen, she was considered the ruler of England. She soon became an unpopular figure, however, because she imposed heavy taxes on the nobles and the citizens of London. Stephen's queen, also named Matilda, rallied support to her husband's cause, and the Lady of the English was driven from London. Stephen was released from prison and returned to the throne in November 1141.

Stephen's troubles, however, did not end there. Those who were loyal to Matilda and Robert continued to challenge his rule for the next eight years. Robert died in 1147 and Matilda retired to Anjou in 1148, never to return, but the civil war dragged on in scattered skirmishes before petering out in 1149. The final blows to Stephen's reign came in 1153 when his eldest son Eustace died. Henry of Anjou, the son of Matilda and Geoffrey Plantagenet, brought an army to England to force Stephen to recognize Henry's claim to the throne. Through the Treaty of Wallingford, Stephen designated Henry as his heir and successor. Stephen died less than a year later.

The House of Anjou

With the death of Stephen in 1154, Henry of Anjou took the throne as Henry II, establishing the House of Anjou that would rule England for the next three hundred years. Henry (reigned 1154–1189) came to the throne of England already as ruler of a significant portion of France. He ruled the provinces of Anjou, Maine, and Normandy as well as Aquitaine through his marriage to Eleanor of Aquitaine. His Angevin realm (the lands ruled by the House of Anjou) stretched from the Scots border in the north to the Pyrenees Mountains in the south, where the modern nations of France and Spain meet.

Henry was a formidable figure with tremendous energy. A contemporary chronicler, Giraldus Cambrensis, wrote that he had "a reddish complexion, his eyes were grey, bloodshot and flashed with anger. He had a fiery countenance, his voice was tremulous, and his neck bent a little forward. . . . He had an enor-

mous paunch, rather by fault of nature than from gross feeding [for] in all things he was moderate, even parsimonious [frugal]."[6]

While Henry's appetite for food may have been moderate, his quest for power was not. He destroyed many of the castles that had been built during the civil war to eliminate their possible use by rivals to challenge his rule and introduced a new code of laws. All local courts, run by the landowning barons, became subordinate to a new central court, which featured a jury system.

The king was less successful, however, in ruling his own family. Henry and Eleanor had eight children, but they did not always agree in matters concerning their offspring. As their four surviving sons reached maturity (one died in infancy) and began to seek a role in the empire, their ambitions became part of a three-sided political game between their parents and each other. Henry bestowed favors on one son at the expense of the others, and Eleanor encouraged schemes by her other sons in order to remain connected to the power of the throne. Her power plays resulted in Henry exiling her from his court in 1167, allowing only occasional visits to her children on holidays, while Henry dallied with a series of mistresses both in England and in France, where he spent most of his later life.

Henry had intended to divide his empire among his sons, but fate and politics intervened. The first son died as a child; the second, Henry (known as the "Young King" since he was the heir apparent) died at age twenty-eight; and the third son, Geoffrey, was killed in an accident in 1186. Geoffrey's death left only sons Richard and John. Richard, the elder son, was Eleanor's favorite, and John was Henry's. Richard formed an alliance with Philip II, the king of France, to invade Henry's French domains, but Henry, prematurely aged at fifty-six, had no energy to fight. The two kings negotiated a peace on July 4, 1189, in which Henry was forced to surrender disputed territories and to acknowledge Richard as his heir. Henry became heartbroken when he discovered that his son John had also been with Philip's forces, and he died of a massive hemorrhage of a stomach ulcer two days later.

Richard I "the Lionheart" (reigned 1189–1199)

Upon his father's death, Richard was crowned king on July 6, 1189. At thirty-one, he retained the youthful vigor that had made him almost a legend. He had been trained as a knight and loved the thrill of the tournament, in which men faced single opponents in contests of strength and skill with a variety of weapons, such as the sword and the lance. He had also gained a reputation as a skilled warrior in a variety of campaigns before becoming king.

Richard ruled from 1189 to 1199, yet spent only six months of that time in England itself. In December 1189 he joined the Third Crusade, arriving in the Holy Land in 1191, but his personality rubbed many of the crusading nobility the wrong way, including one of his allies, Leopold V, Duke of Austria. Richard's army, with the help of Leopold's and the French armies, had broken a two-year siege of the town of Acre but failed to recapture Jerusalem from the Islamic armies. England, Austria, and France had all claimed Acre, but Richard had removed Leopold's banner from the town. Leopold, outraged, returned to Europe. Richard's reputation continued to grow as he proved himself both fearless on the battlefield and an innovative leader, gaining the nickname *Coeur de Lion*, or "Lionheart."

Richard's fortunes changed, however, when he sailed for home in 1192. He and several companions were shipwrecked on the shores of the Adriatic Sea (between the modern-day Balkans and Italy) and were forced to travel across Europe on foot to reach home. As they crossed Leopold's domain, they were captured; Richard remained in prison for fifteen months while his treasury raised the huge ransom for his release. He eventually returned to England in March 1194. There he found that his brother John, who had been responsible for the French territories, had lost portions of Normandy to Philip II. Richard spent the next five years in France fighting to regain the lost territories and died from wounds sustained in a minor battle there in April 1199.

Today, Richard's prowess on the battlefield is legendary, but historians debate his effectiveness as a king. Historian John Gillingham believes that "by the standards of the day, [Richard] was

Richard I, the Lionheart, ruled England from 1189 to 1199 but only spent six months actually in his kingdom due to his participation in the Third Crusade (1189–1192).

an ideal king, preoccupied above all with the crusade and the defense of his ancestral lands," and calls him a "generous lord and a shrewd politician."[7] Ashley, however, labels him "an extremely arrogant, petulant king, with a vicious temper and a total lack of moral scruples. . . . He was an excellent soldier . . . but was useless at anything else."[8] In any case, according to historians Ralph V. Turner and Richard R. Heiser, he "failed at one of a medieval monarch's fundamental tasks; he died without leaving a son as

his undoubted heir."[9] On his death, the crown passed to his brother John.

John Lackland

John I (reigned 1199–1216) was the youngest and last surviving son of Henry II and Eleanor of Aquitaine. He gained the nickname Lackland because his father had already divided his territories among his other sons by the time John was born. As king, he spent almost a decade mounting one campaign after another in vain attempts to maintain the

Angevin realms against French expansionism. To finance these wars, John imposed a number of heavy taxes on the nobles. The most expensive of these was called *scutage,* which a baron had to pay when he declined military service. Scutage had been imposed eleven times from 1154 to 1199, but John levied it eleven times over the next sixteen years. Paying scutage was soon seen as a measure of a baron's loyalty to the king.

By 1214 the nobles had had enough of John's taxes and military failures. A crushing defeat in France in July and the loss of further territory sent the English barons into open rebellion in May 1215. London soon fell to the rebels and on June 15, John met with the barons at the small town of Runnymede to negotiate a peace. There he signed a document that history remembers as the Great Charter, more commonly known by its Latin name, the Magna Carta. The charter laid out the specific rights and privileges of the king and of the barons and became the basis for the rights of individuals under a government, such as the right to a trial of a jury of one's peers.

Civil war broke out again as John soon ignored the charter's provisions and returned to his heavy-handed rule. The rebels pursued John through eastern England, and during this retreat, he developed dysentery and died on October 18, 1216, leaving his son Henry as his heir. John was forty-six years old; Henry was only nine.

Henry III (reigned 1216–1272)

The young Henry III inherited a kingdom torn by civil war, but he was fortunate to

The Magna Carta

The Great Charter (more commonly known by its Latin name Magna Carta) that was signed by King John and his rebellious barons in 1215 was designed to put a variety of limits on the power of the king. The barons felt that John had overstepped the bounds of royal authority. Their intent was to force John to acknowledge restrictions on the king's ability to levy taxes, to respect England's traditional laws and customs, and to recognize a committee that was designed to hold him to that promise.

Over the centuries that followed, the Magna Carta has been touted as an example of the idea that both those who are governed and those who govern must obey the law. Its clauses include a number of concepts that still exist in modern law, such as the prohibition against unlawful imprisonment, the right to a speedy trial, and the right to a trial by a jury of one's peers.

have two effective advisers as his reign began. Hubert de Burgh, Earl of Kent, and William Marshal, Earl of Pembroke, served as the king's regents; they were empowered to act in the king's name during Henry's youth. Marshal and Burgh succeeded in quelling the civil war by 1219. Marshal died that year and Burgh became the sole regent until 1227. Burgh had served Henry's three predecessors ably, but under his regency, the duchy of Aquitaine was lost to France.

Burgh relinquished his role as regent when Henry turned nineteen, and by 1234 Henry had taken on all the traditional roles of kingship. After he married Eleanor, the daughter of the count

Henry III's fifty-six-year reign was marked by treaties with Scotland and Wales and the establishment of a parliament.

of Provence in 1236, he filled his circle of advisers with her relatives and his friends from France. This angered many of the English barons, who wished the king would listen to them instead. The French influence, however, had a remarkable effect on England. At the time, French culture was flowering, and its influence on English music, literature, and architecture remains to this day. Many of the famous Gothic churches that dot today's English landscape, with their soaring towers and huge, arched stained-glass windows, date from this period. At Henry's direction, London's Westminster Abbey was restored and expanded in the Gothic style to honor Henry's patron saint, Edward the Confessor.

Henry's long reign of fifty-six years was also marked by a series of international treaties, which demonstrated that he was more successful at making peace than war. The Treaty of York in 1237 established a strong alliance with Scotland and essentially established the current border between England and Scotland. A similar treaty in 1247 created an alliance with Wales. But the Treaty of Paris in 1259 was less favorable to England. Henry's efforts to restore control over Henry II's Angevin realm failed, and he renounced all English claims to Normandy, Maine, and Anjou.

By this time Henry's relationship with the nobles had deteriorated into open hostility. Over the years he had affirmed their rights under the Magna Carta, only to continue to rule as he wished. In 1258 he agreed to meet with them in a council, called Parliament, to be held three times a year to reform how the realm was ruled. Henry used these meetings to divide his opposition through promises of rewards and, with the support of the pope, the threat of excommunication from the church. The king's ambitious brother-in-law, Simon de Montfort, became the leader of the barons and led them in an open revolt in April 1264 in an attempt to curb royal power. His forces defeated Henry's in May and captured the king and his family. The barons, led by Montfort, issued a call for a new Parliament to include elected representatives from across England. This new body forced Henry over the next year to agree to a series of reforms to royal power. In July 1265, however, Henry's eldest son, Edward, escaped from custody, raised an army, and attacked and defeated the nobles. Henry nullified Parliament's measures and took revenge on his enemies but then negotiated the Treaty of Marlborough in 1267 to spell out baronial rights and privileges.

The Last Angevin or First Plantagenet?

By 1267 Henry III was sixty years old, in declining health, and beginning to suffer from dementia. He died in November 1272. His son Edward became king on Henry's death.

Some historians label Henry III, the great-grandson of Geoffrey of Anjou, as the last Angevin king of England; others style him the first Plantagenet king. Regardless of the designation, Henry III's legacy is unlike that of many of his predecessors. It does not rest on the intangibles of skill on the battlefield but in the tangible Gothic architecture that still exists today. As British historian Peter Earle notes, "Perhaps we give too much glory to our martial kings and too little to those, like Henry III, who have made England a more civilized country."[10]

Chapter Two

The Plantagenets
and the Wars
of the Roses

When Henry III died in 1272, his kingdom had been at peace for three years. At that time his son Edward was on his way home from a crusade. During Edward's leisurely trip back to England, he particpated in celebrations in honor of his role as a hero of the crusade and as the new king. He reached England on August 2, 1274, and his coronation as Edward I took place seventeen days later. His ascension marked the beginning of over one hundred years of kings from the Plantagenet descendants of the House of Anjou.

"The Hammer of the Scots"

Because of his father's long reign, Edward I (reigned 1272–1307) had the good fortune to mature in the role of heir apparent. He already had a record of military accomplishments, but one of his longest-lasting achievements as king was the reformation of the nation's legal system. Commoners and nobles alike benefited as the rights and obligations of landowners were codified. Edward commissioned a thorough survey of the country to resolve disputes over who owned the lands across the realm, which clarified tax collections. He met regularly with Parliament, which after 1295 was composed of the House of Lords (landowners and church leaders) and the House of Commons (elected representatives from the townsfolk and county dwellers). With Parliament's assistance, Edward instituted further reforms over a period of twenty years. According to Mike Ashley, "During this process Edward was quick to punish those who had abused their authority. In this way Edward endeared himself to the commoners of England, who saw him as their saviour."[11]

The commoners and the nobles of Scotland and Wales saw Edward in a much different light. The people of

Wales held him responsible for the loss of their independence. At Edward's coronation, the Welsh leader Llywelyn ap Gruffydd, refused to appear to pay homage (in other words, to acknowledge Edward as his king). In 1267, under the Treaty of Montgomery, Henry III had recognized Llywelyn as the Prince of Wales; as such, Llywelyn believed that he need not pay homage to Edward.

English commoners and nobles alike benefitted from Edward I's reign. However, expanding his kingdom came at the expense of the Welsh and Scots.

Edward felt otherwise and led two campaigns against Llywelyn and his followers in 1277 and 1282. Llywelyn was killed in the second confrontation, and Welsh resistance soon crumbled. The Statute of Wales in 1284 brought the territory into Edward's dominion, and he ordered the construction of a ring of castles to protect it. Many of them stand to this day.

While the Welsh resented Edward for their loss of independence, he was despised by the Scots. In 1286 Edward was invited to mediate a dispute between the three claimants to the vacant Scots throne. Although, according to Peter Earle, his choice was one "which most historians have considered fair and just,"[12] he decided to take advantage of the situation by demanding that the Scots recognize him as their overlord. By 1296 the situation had deteriorated into open warfare. In March 1296 Edward stormed and sacked the town of Berwick, and in April the main Scots army was crushed at the Battle of Dunbar. He accepted the homage of the Scots barons and gained the nickname the Hammer of the Scots.

These defeats led to the rise of two of Scotland's iconic leaders, William Wallace and Robert the Bruce. Wallace led a ragtag army of peasants and outlaws through several campaigns of guerrilla warfare against Edward's army, which defeated him at Falkirk in 1298. In 1307 Robert the Bruce's bid for power led Edward, now sixty-eight, to march north with another army to subdue the Scots. He never got there; he developed dysen-tery and died in sight of the Scots border on July 7, 1307.

Edward II (reigned 1307–1327)

The new king, Edward II, had little of his father's panache. In fact, his twenty-year reign was marked by a series of failures. The country experienced widespread famine due to repeated bouts of severe weather and poor harvests. England's military fortunes suffered in France and in Scotland; a disastrous defeat at the hands of Robert the Bruce at the Battle of Bannockburn in 1314 remains an iconic loss to this day. Edward could not be blamed for the weather, but he could be blamed for the loss to the Scots.

Edward's greatest failure, however, came in the political arena. He was so close to two friends, Piers Gaveston and Hugh Despenser, that contemporary accounts suggest he had sexual relationships with them. While his marriage to Isabella, the daughter of the king of France, resulted in four children, their births were sandwiched between the relationships with Gaveston and Despenser. Edward showered Gaveston with lavish gifts and property even before he became king until a group of nobles, offended by the relationship, forced the king to exile Gaveston twice in three years. After his return to England in early 1312, Gaveston was arrested and executed for treason the following June. The king repeated this behavior with Despenser and Despenser's father, one of the royal advisers. By 1324 Isabella had had enough.

By then her brother ruled France, and under the guise of trying to mend English relations with him, Isabella sailed to Europe. There she began an extramarital affair with Roger Mortimer, a leading member of the anti-Despenser faction. She was joined by her eldest son, Edward, and in September 1326, she, her son, and Mortimer led an army to England. Popular support for the king quickly faded away; one by one, the Despensers and their allies were captured and executed. The king was arrested in November; on January 20, 1327, the lords in Parliament sentenced him to life in prison, and four days later he abdicated in favor of his son. He was later executed, possibly on the orders of Isabella or Mortimer. It was an ignominious end to a troubled reign.

Edward III

Upon his father's abdication, fourteen-year-old Edward III (reigned 1327–1377) embarked on an historic fifty-year reign. Fortunately, he was more like his grandfather than his father. His leadership skills led to a period of rare internal peace with the English nobles and historically significant military victories in Scotland and France.

Edward III spent much of his time campaigning in France. In 1346 he defeated Philip VI of France at the Battle of Crécy, depicted here.

Edward first led English forces against Scotland in 1327. His army's skill with a new weapon, the longbow, brought him an overwhelming victory at Halidon Hill in 1333. He also became embroiled in a succession crisis in France, when its king, Charles IV, who was Edward's uncle, died without a male heir in 1328. Although Edward believed he had a legitimate claim to the crown, he bided his time for several years. He cultivated antagonism toward the French among his people and his nobles, and in 1338 he began a series of campaigns that opened what is now called the Hundred Years' War. His most important victory of that war came at Crécy in 1346, where once again his longbowmen were the key to winning the battle.

Edward's success in raising money and men for these expensive campaigns was due to his excellent relations with his nobles. His court was modeled on the mythical King Arthur's Knights of the Round Table, in which chivalry and cooperation were tantamount. He invited Europe's greatest knights to his court to test their strength and courage at his tournaments, which spread England's prestige far and wide.

The Black Death

In 1348 a disease swept across Edward's dominion that brought a pall over his reign and the prestige of his court. England and the rest of Europe were ravaged by the bubonic plague, a deadly sickness that was also known as the Black Death. Henry Knighton, a fourteenth-century cleric, recorded that the disease first hit southern England: "Then the dreadful pestilence made its way along the coast by Southampton and reached Bristol, where almost the whole strength of the town perished, as it were surprised by sudden death; for few kept their beds [were ill] more than two or three days, or even half a day. Then this cruel death spread on all sides, following the course of the sun [from east to west]."[13]

The plague killed both the rich and the poor without discrimination. Edward lost a teenage daughter and an infant son to the disease. Across England from 1348 to 1350, one-third of the population, close to a million people, died from it. Crops and animals died because there was no one to tend them. Widespread poverty, famine, and ruin followed, as families, neighborhoods, and entire villages succumbed. Just when the plague seemed to have disappeared, it returned in 1360 as Edward was again campaigning in France. It so weakened his army that he finally sought peace with the enemy.

For the next seventeen years, Edward III's reign was a period of steady decline. Military losses in France and the deaths of his eldest son and his wife left him demoralized and unable to rule effectively. When he died in 1377 the throne passed to his eldest son's ten-year-old child, Richard. Richard II (reigned 1377–1399) encouraged the development of cultural pursuits, including literature, and it was during his reign that Geoffrey Chaucer wrote the *Canterbury Tales* (1387). But Richard's reign was a turbulent twenty-two years, beset by revolts over taxation and internal squabbles between nobles. His staunchest supporter was his uncle, John of Gaunt, Duke of Lancaster. He was the head of the Lancaster branch of the Plantagenets and the premier lord in England, second only in power to the king. John's son, Henry Bolingbroke, however, opposed Edward, and when John of Gaunt died in 1399, Bolingbroke moved against the king. He captured Richard, imprisoned him, and forced him to abdicate in his favor. Thus Bolingbroke was crowned King Henry IV on October 13, 1399.

The Reign of the House of Lancaster

Henry IV reigned from 1399 to 1413. He was keenly sensitive to threats to his rule; in the words of historian Miri Rubin, "The usurper [someone who takes the throne without the right to it, often by force] was rightly alert to the many possibilities which endangered him; usurpers are open to usurpation, and this became the keynote of Henry IV's reign."[14] In the first few years on the throne, he and his supporters successfully suppressed several challenges and plots against him. He was supported by a core group of allies and by the wealth of the House of Lancaster, amassed by his father. As he stabilized the political landscape of England and quashed rebellions in Wales, Henry gained more support among his subjects.

Although Henry's place on the throne was secure, he was by no means at peace. The members of Parliament often

Katherine of Valois and Owain Tudor

After the untimely death of Henry V in 1422, his widow, Katherine of Valois, began a secret relationship with a Welshman named Owain Tudor. Little is known about Tudor's early life; he was born around 1400 to a family descended from a Welsh prince. One story says that he was one of the Welsh bowmen in Henry V's army at Agincourt in 1415 and that the king rewarded him with a place at his court, although he would have been quite young for such an honor. But the records agree that following Henry V's death, he was in the king's household and came to the attention of the widowed queen.

It was forbidden by English law for the king's widow to marry without the (new) king's permission, but Katherine and Tudor apparently defied this dictum by living together, if not marrying in secret, from 1428 until Katherine's death in 1437. By then, they had had at least five children. One of them, Edmund, was the father of Henry Tudor, the future Henry VII.

Henry V's army won a stunning victory at the Battle of Agincourt in 1415, depicted here. Henry was recognized as the heir to the French throne by the Treaty of Troyes in 1419.

took issue with his demands for funds for his military campaigns, and while he usually reacted moderately to avoid any confrontation that might cost him the throne, the stress took a toll. By 1411 he was suffering from a strange wasting disease that left him badly disfigured; he died in March 1413, with his heir apparent, Prince Henry, at his side.

The chronicler Thomas Walsingham notes that Henry IV "for thirteen and a half years less five days reigned gloriously."[15] The reign of his son, however, remains one of the most famous in British history. Henry V ruled for just nine years (reigned 1413–1422), but during that time he focused his single-minded resolve on pressing English claims to the throne of France. He received the support of both Parliament and the people and invaded France in August 1415, reigniting the Hundred Years' War. On October 25, his army, outnumbered perhaps three to one, won a stunning victory at Agincourt. Four thousand Frenchmen, including many nobles, died in the battle, compared with just four hundred of Henry's army.

It took another four years of fighting before Henry was recognized as the heir to the French throne by the Treaty of Troyes. He married Katherine of Valois, the daughter of the king of France, and they had a son, also called Henry, in 1421. But during the following summer, once again campaigning in France, Henry took ill and died, likely from dysentery. By a quirk of fate, the French king died shortly thereafter. Historians and amateurs alike speculate what might have happened if Henry V had lived to wear the crowns of both England and France. Instead, his nine-month-old son was thrust into that role.

Henry VI (reigned 1422–1461 and 1470–1471)

When Henry V died, England was still recovering from the ravages of the previous century's outbreaks of the Black Death. Villages remained empty and decaying, and towns that had bustled with commerce struggled to survive. The wool trade had been decimated by a disease that wiped out entire flocks. By the time Henry VI died, however, English traders were again successfully selling their wares throughout Europe.

The infant Henry VI was raised by a series of nurses, tutors, and religious educators, as well as many trusted household servants from Henry V's staff. His mother, Queen Katherine, lived with her son and helped coordinate his few public appearances before the age of seven, before establishing her own household and secretly marrying a Welshman named Owain Tudor. Henry VI's coronation on November 6, 1429, was a formality; England continued to be ruled by a council of men designated in Henry V's will.

The young king declared himself of age in November 1437, just before his sixteenth birthday. Unfortunately, Henry VI's rule was not as successful as his father's. The new king was unlike his father in many ways. In Ashley's opinion, "Henry VI is a prime example of the wrong king at the wrong time, and that made for a very tragic reign."[16] During his reign, England lost battle after battle in France and more and more territory. When the Hundred Years' War finally ended in 1453 with the French victory at Castillon, the only part of France left in English hands was the port of Calais.

Later that year the king suffered his first attack of a debilitating mental illness. The condition may have been inherited from his maternal grandfather, the king of France, who had been prone to fits of madness. Months passed as Henry sat expressionless in a deep depression. When he recovered, he had no memory of the passage of time. His only son was born during his first bout; when he emerged from the melancholia eighteen months later, he did not recognize the boy or remember anything about his birth.

During this and later episodes, a struggle for power ensued. The king's chief adviser, Edmund Beaufort, Duke of Somerset, was opposed by Richard Plantagenet, Duke of York. York was

The Mystery of Edward IV's Sons

During Richard III's quest for the throne in 1483, he succeeded in removing Edward IV's two young sons, the heir apparent Edward (twelve years old) and Prince Richard (nine years old), from public view by setting them up in the Tower of London. The king's nephews were seen playing in the tower grounds from time to time during the summer of 1483, but then the sightings stopped. The princes were never seen in public again.

The mystery surrounding their fates is tied to Richard's assuming the throne. In those bloody days of winner-take-all politics, it is unlikely that Richard would have let the princes survive as rallying points for his opponents. Contemporary observers and historians agree that the boys were likely murdered, perhaps on their uncle's orders. In 1674 workers rebuilding part of the tower came across two skeletons in a wooden box, which were thought to be those of the princes. They were reinterred in Westminster Abbey. In 1933 the bones were examined by leading British forensic experts, who agreed that they belonged to two young males, approximately thirteen and eleven years old. Since then, the skeletons have lain undisturbed, although current DNA science could shed more light on whose bones they were.

This nineteenth-century lithograph depicts the murder of two of Edward IV's sons. It is believed that their uncle, Richard III, had hatched the plot.

descended through ancestors and marriage from three sons of Edward III, so many of his supporters felt that he was entitled to the throne and would make a better king than Henry. Parliament named him Protector of the Realm in 1454, to act in Henry's name until Henry recovered his health. This emboldened York to imprison Somerset, but the king recovered in 1455 and freed Somerset and stripped York of his title. According to Rubin, "This was a test of York's ambition and loyalty. Would he step down and accept a more modest political role? He did not."[17] York's ambition led to the first skirmish of what historians call the Wars of the Roses.

The Wars of the Roses

Over the next thirty years, England was beset by intermittent fighting between the allies of Henry VI's House of Lancaster and the House of York. This conflict between two related branches of the Plantagenet dynasty came to be known as the Wars of the Roses. The name refers to symbols often used by the two houses. The Lancastrians used red roses; the Yorkists used white. At its heart, these were feuds between two families and their supporters, with the prize being the throne.

The conflicts began in May 1455 with a battle between the Lancastrians and the Yorkists at St. Albans. The Yorkists won the battle, and Somerset was killed. The Duke of York did not try to seize power afterward; instead, he regained his position of protector when King Henry's health declined again. In 1456

Henry's queen, Margaret of Anjou, gained the support of his advisers to rule in his stead, and York was removed for a second time. Margaret despised York and encouraged the new Duke of Somerset, Henry Beaufort, to support her and the king as his father had done. Meanwhile, York gained the support of Richard Neville, the Earl of Salisbury, and his son (also named Richard), the Earl of Warwick.

In 1459 the civil war erupted again. This time the Lancastrians won at the Battle of Ludlow, and York and Warwick were forced into exile. Warwick returned the following year and defeated the Lancastrians, enabling York to press his claim to the throne before Parliament. The Act of Accord recognized York as Henry's heir apparent. Henry's queen, Margaret, understandably objected, as it disinherited her son. She gathered an army of supporters in the north and defeated the Yorkists in December 1460; both York and Salisbury were killed. She marched south to London, defeated Warwick at the second battle of St. Albans, and liberated the king from Yorkist London. Warwick and York's son Edward retook London three months later, in March 1461, and Edward declared himself king. Henry and Margaret fled north, pursued by Edward and Warwick; the two armies clashed at Towton, a village in the northern county of Yorkshire, on March 29, 1461, in the middle of a snowstorm. The Lancastrians were defeated and Henry and Margaret sought refuge in Scotland.

Edward and Warwick

Following the Yorkist victory at Towton, Edward of York began his reign as Edward IV (reigned 1461–1470 and 1471–1483). The deposed queen, meanwhile, tried to enlist support to have Henry returned to the throne, but to no avail. After three years, Henry sneaked back into England, hoping to raise an army. He spent a year incognito in the north until he was caught by Edward's supporters in July 1465 and imprisoned in the Tower of London.

During Henry's exile, Edward became a level-headed ruler and an able administrator. He encouraged English merchants to trade overseas, generating income and prosperity for his nation. The end of war with France eliminated expensive military campaigns. Soon Edward's treasury became solvent, which led to the reduction or elimination of burdensome taxes. All of this increased Edward's popularity.

Edward, however, made a significant mistake by antagonizing the Earl of Warwick. For supporting Edward, Warwick had been rewarded with the post of chamberlain of England, becoming the second-most powerful man in the land. He negotiated a political marriage between the king and a French princess only to discover that Edward had secretly married a commoner, Elizabeth Woodville. The king had been able to keep the marriage secret for four months; when it became public in September 1464, there was a tremendous public uproar. Not only was this marriage seen as unsuitable because Elizabeth was far below the king in social standing and had no royal blood, but her family had supported the Lancastrians.

Warwick was incensed, but stayed loyal, proposing a variety of marriage contracts between the king's family and his own. Edward refused them all, and when the king arranged for his sister to marry the Duke of Burgundy, Warwick broke with Edward. He gave his support to Edward's brother George, Duke of Clarence, who wanted to be king. Warwick supported a series of rebellions in northern England in 1468, which resulted in Edward's capture in July. Warwick imprisoned the king and tried to rule in his name but had no support in Parliament. He released Edward in October 1469, and the king returned to power with much public acclaim.

Tangled Politics

Warwick realized that he needed help in order to regain his former power. He formed an alliance with Margaret of Anjou, the queen of the imprisoned Henry VI. She was still advocating the Lancastrian cause, with the support of King Louis XI of France. Louis gave Warwick and Margaret an army and a fleet, and they invaded England in September 1470. Edward fled to France. The result was that on October 3, 1470, a puzzled and disheveled Henry, who had, in the words of the chronicler John Blacman, "patiently endured hunger, thirst, mockings, derisions, abuse and many other hardships"[18] in prison, was restored to the throne. Warwick begged the king's forgiveness.

Richard Neville, Earl of Warwick: The Kingmaker

One of the most colorful individuals in the English conflict called the Wars of the Roses was Richard Neville, Earl of Warwick. His actions removed Henry VI, brought Edward IV to the throne, and then oversaw Henry's return. The first historian to describe him as "the kingmaker" was John Major, a Scotsman, who in 1521 wrote a history of Great Britain in which he described Warwick with the Latin phrase *regum creator* (maker of kings) and that "of him, it was said that he made kings and at his pleasure cast them down."

Such actions would be controversial in any century, and indeed he was controversial in his own day. Chroniclers who were sympathetic to the Yorkist cause depicted him as a great man, popular with the nation, but driven to his actions by the betrayal of his friend King Edward. Others were less generous. As early as 1471, the year he was killed at the Battle of Barnet, a character study portrayed him as a man driven by ego and a lust for power. Since then, historians have tried to reconcile these two views into an accurate depiction of the man and his motives.

Quoted in Michael A. Hicks. *Warwick the Kingmaker*. Oxford, UK: Blackwell, 1998, p. 3.

Henry's return to the throne, however, was short-lived. Edward gained an army from his brother-in-law, the Duke of Burgundy, landed in England in March 1471, and outmaneuvered Warwick to enter London in April. Two days later, Henry and Warwick fled the capital. Edward's forces caught up with them, Warwick was killed, and Henry was imprisoned once more. Margaret returned from France with an invasion force in May. Her army was defeated and her son Edward was slain. The former queen was imprisoned. Edward spared her life but had Henry executed on May 21, 1471.

The last years of Edward IV's reign were anticlimactic. The land began to prosper again. By 1482 the athletic soldier-turned-king had declined into a stout and inactive middle-aged man. He contracted a fever and died on April 9, 1483, just short of his forty-first birthday. The throne passed to his twelve-year-old son, Edward; in his will the king had named his brother Richard of Gloucester as protector.

The Fall of the House of York

Edward was in Wales when his father died. As he made his way to London, he was met by his uncle Richard, who professed his loyalty to the young heir. It was most certainly a lie, as he quickly moved to ensure that he himself would assume the throne. He set up Edward and his younger brother in the Tower of London, which had served as a royal residence as well as prison since the days of William the Conqueror. With the young princes firmly controlled, Richard had Edward IV's marriage to Elizabeth Woodville declared invalid, based on an alleged marriage contract that predated the king's marriage to Woodville. No evidence of this contract was ever produced, but Parliament accepted the allegations and declared any children from the marriage illegitimate. That placed Richard of Gloucester next in line to the throne, and he was declared King Richard III on June 26, 1483. It had taken him just nine weeks to remove the legitimate heir and become king.

As it turned out, he was king for a rather short time, from 1483 to 1485. Elizabeth Woodville, who was afraid she would never see her sons again, entered into an alliance with a Welshman, Henry Tudor. She agreed that, in exchange for Henry's support against Richard, Henry could marry her daugh-

Richard III (left) was slain at the Battle of Bosworth Field. He was the last English monarch to die in battle.

ter Elizabeth. Henry Tudor was the grandson of Owain Tudor and Katherine of Valois, Henry V's widow, and as such was the last surviving Lancastrian; now, he was set to marry the daughter of the late Yorkist king. In the words of historian Anthony Cheetham, "The Wars of the Roses created some strange bedfellows."[19]

Tudor methodically assembled an army while Richard waited impatiently to face him. Tudor landed his army on August 7, 1485, in South Wales, and met Richard's army near the village of Market Bosworth in the English county of Leicestershire. Richard was so intent in putting down this insurrection and killing Tudor that he rode his horse into the thick of the fighting and was slain.

Richard III was the last English king to die in battle. Because his only legitimate son had died in 1484, his death at Bosworth Field meant the Plantagenets were no more. Henry Tudor, a Welshman who had spent most of his life in exile as a Lancastrian opponent to Yorkist rule, was now proclaimed the king of England. Five months later, he married Edward IV's daughter Elizabeth. The marriage united the houses of Lancaster and York and brought the Wars of the Roses to an end. To commemorate this union, Henry's design for the new royal dynasty, called the House of Tudor, was a red and white rose.

Chapter Three

The House of Tudor

When Henry Tudor was crowned on August 22, 1485, after his victory in the last battle of the Wars of the Roses at Bosworth Field, observers could have been excused for thinking that his was merely another chapter in the battles between the houses of York and Lancaster. Henry, the head of the Lancastrians, was succeeding Richard III of the House of York.

Henry's claim to the throne was certainly not as strong as Richard's had been. He was a descendant of Edward III's son, John of Gaunt, and his mistress Katherine Swynford. Their son, John Beaufort, had been named Duke of Somerset, and Beaufort's granddaughter was Henry's mother. Henry was also descended from Welsh princes, but his true claim to the throne was as William the Conqueror's had been: through conquest. The former king was dead, and Henry Tudor became Henry VII.

The First Tudor King

Henry VII (reigned 1485–1509) soon received support from two very important institutions in English life: Parliament and the Catholic Church. In November 1485 Parliament convened in London to proclaim him the legitimate king of England. The following January, Pope Innocent VIII declared Henry the rightful ruler of the land and threatened anyone who opposed him with excommunication from the church. Despite this support, individuals challenged Henry's rule, but he thwarted each of them. Some opponents were imprisoned, and some were executed, but others were pardoned. One of these opponents, Lambert Simnel, who claimed to be a son of Edward IV, was just a teenager. Henry found him a job in the royal kitchens instead of imprisoning him.

As the years passed, Henry succeeded in establishing goodwill with other nations and ushering in a period of domestic calm in England—something that had been a rarity for generations. He forged a peace treaty with Scotland in 1502; his daughter Margaret married the Scots king James IV the following year. He also agreed to a marriage between his firstborn son, Arthur, and Catherine of Aragon when the boy was just three years old. Catherine was the daughter of the king and queen of Spain,

King Henry VIII was a natural athlete, a fine horseman, and an accomplished linguist, musician, and composer. He would be remembered for redefining the role of religion and royalty in England.

and the agreement helped foster mutual goodwill between England and one of the richest nations in Europe.

England's finances were also improving. Henry kept tight control of government expenditures, and commerce flourished as the threat of further civil war receded. But Henry personally was not at peace. His wife, Elizabeth, died in childbirth in 1501; his eldest son, Arthur, died childless the following year at age sixteen. Henry kept more and more to himself, suffered from gout and asthma, and died in 1509 at age fifty-two. As Mike Ashley puts it, "Personally Henry was a sad king . . . perhaps never truly enjoying the success that he achieved."[20]

Henry VIII (reigned 1509–1547)

Upon the death of Henry VII, his third child and second son, Henry, became king. The now teenaged Henry had become the heir apparent when his older brother Arthur had died in 1502, and he was two months shy of his eighteenth birthday when his father died. The dying king wished for Henry to marry Arthur's widow, Catherine of Aragon, in order to continue the alliance with Spain. The wedding took place six weeks after Henry VII's death.

Henry was quite unlike his father in many ways. The old king was dour and reserved; the new king was outgoing and jovial. As a prince Henry had enjoyed touring the land and meeting with the people. He was a natural athlete, a fine horseman, and an accomplished linguist, musician, and composer. But these skills and accomplishments are rarely why Henry VIII is remembered, and they are not why he remains one of England's most iconic kings. Instead, he is most often remembered for a personal problem that he and his advisers called his "great matter." This personal problem rocked the nation and redefined the role of the religion and royalty in England.

The King's Great Matter

For the first few years of Henry's reign, his marriage to his brother's widow, Catherine of Aragon, seemed untroubled. They had a daughter, Mary, in 1516, but also had five other children that did not survive. After ten years of marriage, Henry believed that Catherine was incapable of bearing him a healthy son. This was reinforced when Henry's mistress, Bessie Blount, bore a healthy boy in 1519. Henry grew uninterested in his wife. Increasingly convinced that God was cursing him for marrying his brother's wife, he began to seek a divorce.

Henry and his counselors tried to convince Pope Clement VII that the marriage should be dissolved, but Clement was heavily influenced by the Spanish king, Charles V, who was Catherine's nephew. The matter dragged on for years, and it was compounded by the appearance of a young woman at Henry's court named Anne Boleyn. Henry pursued her fervently, but she refused to become his mistress. Just before Christmas 1526, after eighteen months of the chase, he declared to Anne in a letter,

The King's Troubles

New scientific theories shed light on the troubles that Henry VIII had in producing a male heir. In 2011 two scientists suggested that the root of the problem may have been Henry's blood type.

In an age when many children did not survive past infancy, the king and his various partners were famously unlucky, with several pregnancies resulting in miscarriages or stillborn births. Biological archaeologist Catarina Whitley and anthropologist Kyra Kramer theorize that Henry may have belonged to a rare blood group called "Kell positive."

Only 9 percent of Caucasians belong to this group. When a Kell positive man and a Kell negative woman try to have children, the first birth is usually normal. However, during pregnancy or at birth, some of the baby's blood will mingle with the mother's blood, leading her blood to produce antibodies that will attack later concentrations of Kell positive blood, such as in subsequent pregnancies. This new theory fits the contemporary evidence of the pregnancies of the king's maternal great-grandmother, her descendants, and Henry VIII and his wives.

"If it pleases you to do the duty of a true, loyal mistress and friend, and to give yourself body and heart to me, who had been and will be your very loyal servant, I promise that not only the name will be due to you but also to take you as my sole mistress, casting off all others than yourself out of mind and affection and to serve you and you alone."[21] But Anne had no wish to be just the king's mistress. She wanted to be queen.

As the papal court refused to resolve the "great matter"—that is, the pursuit of a divorce from one woman in order to marry another who might bear him an heir—in Henry's favor, both he and his ministers began to feel that the only way he could end his marriage with Catherine was to take matters into his own hands. Henry had been a loyal Catholic his entire life. When protesters in Europe began to clamor for reforms to many of the church's practices, such as the practice of granting salvation in return for monetary payments, Henry had defended the church. As this movement, which came to be called the Protestant Reformation, gained support from all walks of life across Europe, however, Henry recognized an opportunity to resolve his problem. He persuaded Parliament to declare that he, and not the pope, was the supreme head of the church in England. In so doing, the king and government officially broke from the Catholic Church. The proclamation enabled Henry, in essence, to grant his own divorce. Catherine was banished from court and lived out the rest of her days in Cambridgeshire, never wavering in her Catholic faith, until her death in 1536.

Henry and Anne Boleyn were married in a secret ceremony in January 1533, and she was crowned queen the following spring. She was already pregnant. She and the king were convinced that she would have a son, but the healthy child was a girl, whom they named Elizabeth when she was born on September 7, 1533. They believed that a son would follow, but two additional children were stillborn, including a boy in 1536. Henry's melancholy over the inability to produce a legitimate heir deepened, and he began to listen to whispered accusations of Anne's infidelity and practice of witchcraft. Henry finally had her arrested on charges of adultery and treason, and she was beheaded on May 19, 1536, after a turbulent decade as the object of Henry's desire. She had been queen for only a thousand days.

Jane Seymour, Anne of Cleves, and Catherine Howard

A new queen was in the wings to take Anne's place. Henry's roving eye had fallen upon Jane Seymour, the daughter of one of his knights. Seymour had learned from Anne's successes and failures; she was demure and reserved instead of ostentatious and outspoken as Anne had been, but she, too, wished to be Henry's wife and not his mistress.

They were married just eleven days after Anne's execution, and she was proclaimed queen in June. Henry was forty-six; Jane was twenty-five.

By the following spring, Jane was pregnant, and on October 12, 1537, she gave birth to a healthy boy whom they named Edward after his great-great-grandfather. The pregnancy so weakened Jane that she fell ill two days after his birth and died ten days later. Henry was devastated by her death, but he now had the male heir he had so desperately wanted.

The king remained without a queen for more than two years until he agreed to a political marriage that would strengthen his ties to Protestant rulers in Germany. He assented to a marriage to Anne of Cleves after viewing a flattering portrait of her. When she arrived in England in January 1540, however, he was repulsed by her appearance. The marriage went ahead anyway, but lasted only seven months before both agreed to a divorce. Henry was generous in the settlement, and he and Anne remained friends afterwards.

Henry's next choice for a wife—now his fifth—was a young woman named Catherine Howard, who was perhaps thirty years his junior, as her date of birth is uncertain. She seemed to rejuvenate the king, who had grown quite obese in middle age (he now had a fifty-four-inch waist (137cm). But Catherine soon tired of her husband, and when he discovered she was having adulterous affairs with two old beaus, he had her beheaded on February 13, 1452, after just over eighteen months of marriage.

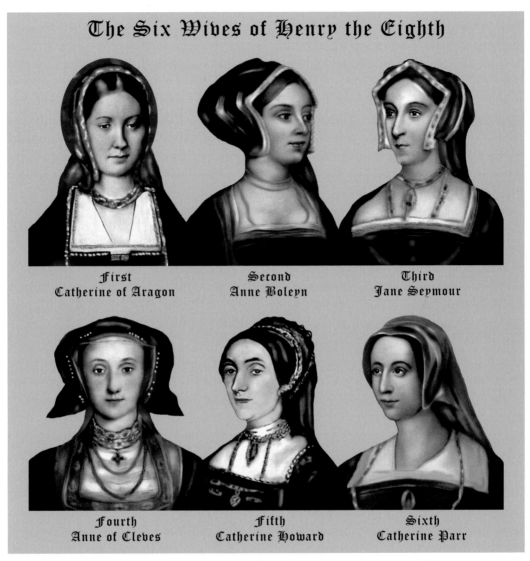

The Six Wives of Henry the Eighth

First
Catherine of Aragon

Second
Anne Boleyn

Third
Jane Seymour

Fourth
Anne of Cleves

Fifth
Catherine Howard

Sixth
Catherine Parr

King Henry VIII broke from the Catholic Church and over the course of his life married six different women.

Henry VIII's Final Years

After all these experiences, many were surprised when Henry decided to get married a sixth time. No one was as surprised as the woman to whom he proposed. Catherine Parr, at thirty-three, was unlike any of his previous wives, particularly as she was twice widowed.

Following their marriage in 1453, Catherine Parr succeeded in reuniting Henry with his children. Mary, still a devout Catholic, and Elizabeth, increasingly Protestant, had been declared illegitimate when Edward was born, but Henry returned them to the inheritance in his later years. The princesses and Edward, an intelligent lad prone to illness, enjoyed their new stepmother, and she helped direct their education for several years.

By this time, Henry was ailing. He had never truly recovered from a leg injury in a riding contest in 1536, and by the end of 1546, he was prematurely aged and knew that his days were coming to a close. In his will, he directed that a council of advisers should act as regent for his heir, the young Edward. He died on January 28, 1547, at age fifty-five.

Henry VIII left behind a complicated legacy. Breaking with the Catholic Church stripped the clergy of much of its wealth and power, but untold thousands of Henry's subjects refused to desert the Church. It had been the foundation of their lives for generations, even longer than allegiance to the king. Henry's actions served him well, as it enriched his treasury and enabled him to change wives at will, but it also divided his people in two: those who were devoted to the original church, and those who were bent on driving it out. He skillfully negotiated a series of alliances with European powers, but was apparently unable to maintain a happy home life. And in the words of historians John Cannon and Ralph Griffiths, "If the primary objective of Henry's policy was to secure the succession, he could hardly have done worse. Six marriages had produced one sickly son, and two princesses, whose inheritance had been placed in jeopardy"[22] by Henry's changing whims.

Part of this contradictory behavior may have been genetic. In 2011 researchers Catarina Whitley and Kyra Kramer suggested that Henry VIII may have carried a genetic disease called McLeod syndrome. It usually sets in around age forty, with symptoms that include heart disease, muscle weakness and fatigue, and psychological symptoms such as paranoia. Whitley and Kramer suggest the syndrome could explain the king's behavioral changes in his later years. "This gives us an alternative way of interpreting Henry and understanding his life," said Whitley. "It gives us a new way to look at the reasons he changed."[23]

Edward VI and Lady Jane Grey

With Henry's death, the young Edward VI (reigned 1547–1553) came to the throne. His uncle, the Earl of Somerset, usurped the late king's plans for a council of regents when he seized power and became the Protector of the Realm. He was succeeded in 1552 by the Earl of Warwick. Under their sway, Edward directed further Protestant reforms, including the Acts of Uniformity of 1549 and 1552, which codified Church of England services. For example, masses conducted in Latin were eliminated in favor of worship directed by the English-language Book of Common Prayer.

These initiatives depended on the support of the staunchly Protestant king. His hope for a Protestant England extended to his will, in which he directed that his Catholic half-sister, Mary, should be passed over in favor of his Protestant cousin Lady Jane Grey, the granddaughter of Henry VIII's youngest sister. This directive became all the more important as Edward's health began to fail in the spring of 1552. He suffered from congenital syphilis inherited from his father and also contracted tuberculosis. He was just fifteen when he died on July 6, 1553.

On July 9 the late king's circle of advisers, known as the Privy Council, offered the throne to Lady Jane Grey. The fifteen-year-old was reluctant to accept but did so in order to continue the Protestant reforms, and she was proclaimed queen the next day. The

King Edward VI directed Protestant reforms but died of tuberculosis at the age of fifteen.

men who had maneuvered Edward into nominating her as heir, and who had then offered the throne to her, had underestimated the populace, however. There was overwhelming support for Mary, and Lady Jane's supporters were promptly defeated. Lady Jane abdicated after just nine days.

Mary I (reigned 1553–1558)

Mary, the daughter of Henry VIII and Catherine of Aragon, was crowned the first queen regnant of England (in other words, the first woman who was not queen because of her marriage to the king) on October 1, 1553. Cannon and Griffiths state that her reign, "which began with so striking a demonstration of loyalty, is the most tragic, publicly and personally, in English history. On the character of Mary, historians differ. What to some is steadfast courage in adversity is to others no more than stubborn bigotry, nor perhaps are the two always far apart."[24]

Mary had been raised a Catholic by her mother and had remained so as the Protestant Reformation swept England. When she became queen, she was thirty-seven and still single. She revoked several of Henry VIII's measures that discriminated against Catholics but felt that returning England completely to the Catholic Church would endanger her rule. She nonetheless sanctioned a campaign of persecution against Protestant reformers, and nearly three hundred were burned at the stake between February 1555 and November 1558. The queen, who had enjoyed such popular support at the start, became known as Bloody Mary.

Mary also lost popular support when she married Philip of Spain, the heir to the Spanish throne, in 1554. She loved him deeply, but her love was not reciprocated; his callous treatment left her depressed and heartbroken. Additionally, she suffered through two false pregnancies in 1554 and 1557. In the fall of 1558, weak and ailing, she grudgingly acknowledged her half-sister Elizabeth as her heir. She died on November 17, 1558, from complications of influenza.

Elizabeth I (reigned 1558–1603)

When Mary died in 1558, Elizabeth became the last surviving child of Henry VIII. Although she barely knew her mother (Anne Boleyn was executed before Elizabeth's third birthday) and spent much of her childhood estranged from her father, she grew into a strong and healthy teen who enjoyed dancing, hunting, riding, and archery. When both Edward and Mary died childless, the twenty-five-year-old Elizabeth inherited the throne. People lit bonfires in celebration and threw parties in the streets to celebrate her ascension.

Despite this popularity, Elizabeth understood that, as a woman, she would be the target of intrigue among the powerful men of her realm. For centuries, female members of royalty were used as pawns to cement political alliances both at home and abroad. The new queen recognized that any marriage, no matter how politically expedient or advan-

When Elizabeth I ascended the throne, she championed the Protestant cause but did not force her Catholic subjects to renounce their religion.

tageous, could lead to jealousy and conspiracy among the nobles. Conversely, she realized that a political marriage was important for producing an heir and strengthening ties in Europe.

The queen had several suitors, both English and European, over the years. She turned down all offers of marriage and by the time her last serious suitor died in 1584, Elizabeth was over fifty and beyond childbearing years. By then, she had been labeled the Virgin Queen, a title in which she delighted, as it suggested that she was putting the nation's needs ahead of her own. And in the early years of her reign, one of the nation's needs was to heal the religious divisions that had arisen during Mary's years.

Protestant Champion

Elizabeth steered a middle course to help heal the rifts between Protestants and

Catholics over which religious practices most accurately interpreted the biblical Gospels. She had no wish to continue the extremes of her siblings. Although she declared that the nation was officially Protestant, she would not, in her words, "open windows in men's souls"[25] and force them to convert. Attendance at Church of England services was enough; if someone wanted to hear the Catholic mass in private, there was no harm in that.

In Rome Pope Pius V was not so tolerant. In 1570 he declared that Elizabeth should be removed from the throne in order to return England to the Catholic Church. Elizabeth wisely ignored the proclamation, but in the minds of many Protestants, the edict effectively changed English Catholics from nonconformists to potential traitors. In their view, one could not be loyal to the monarch (the head of the English church) and to the pope (the head of the Catholic Church) at the same time. To Elizabeth's dismay, Catholic persecution returned as Protestant zealots harassed and injured Catholics across the country, and her ideal middle ground dissolved into extremism.

At the same time, Elizabeth tried to deal with a troublesome cousin who had remained Catholic. The result was the darkest blemish on her forty-five-year-long reign.

Elizabeth and Mary, Queen of Scots

One of the central players in Elizabeth's monarchy was her cousin, Mary, Queen of Scots, a member of Scotland's House of Stuart. Mary was a devout Catholic and, as the granddaughter of Henry VIII's sister, was also Elizabeth's cousin. She had been crowned queen of Scotland in 1543 after her father, King James V, died, but then moved to France when she married the future French king François II. She returned to Scotland after his death in 1561, but by then the Scots Parliament had declared that the nation was Protestant. Mary found herself the cen-

Mary Queen of Scots was found guilty of plotting the assassination of Elizabeth I and was beheaded on February 8, 1587.

The Mystery of the "Lost Colony"

One of the iconic stories of the reign of Queen Elizabeth I is the enduring mystery of the "lost colony" of Roanoke Island. On this small island just west of North Carolina's Outer Banks, more than one hundred men, women, and children attempted to start a new life in the New World in 1587. Their sponsor, Sir Walter Raleigh, and their governor, John White, had intended to plant the colony on the southern banks of Chesapeake Bay. A variety of circumstances, however, obliged them to start their new lives at a military camp on Roanoke Island that Raleigh's men had abandoned the year before.

Poor living conditions forced John White to return to England to petition for more supplies. The threat of war with Spain delayed his return for three years. In 1590 he found the village eerily deserted, with few clues as to the colonists' fate. To this day, no one knows what happened to the men, women, and children of the colony, which included White's daughter, son-in-law, and their child, Virginia Dare. The mystery is commemorated at the Fort Raleigh National Historic Site in Manteo, North Carolina.

ter of several plots connected to Catholic persecution and quests for power.

In 1566 Mary married Lord Darnley in a Catholic ceremony, and that same year she gave birth to a son, James, who was baptized a Catholic. Mary and Darnley were opposed by several Protestant Scots leaders, and Darnley was assassinated. Although Mary later married the Earl of Bothwell in a Protestant ceremony, a group of lords distrusted her conversion to Protestantism. These lords imprisoned Mary, wishing to replace her with her son in hopes of becoming the power behind his throne.

Under duress, Mary abdicated in July 1567 in favor of her one-year-old son, who became King James VI. She escaped from prison the following year and fled to England, hoping that Elizabeth would grant her asylum. She hoped to raise an army and return to Scotland. But fearing that her deposed cousin would become a focal point for Catholic rebellion in England, Elizabeth placed Mary under what amounted to house arrest for the next nineteen years.

English and Scots Catholics tried to plan rebellions in Mary's name, and in 1586 Mary implicated herself in a plot to assassinate Elizabeth in connection with an invasion from Catholic Spain. She was put on trial for her role in the conspiracy and found guilty of treason. Elizabeth reluctantly signed her cousin's death warrant, and Mary, Queen of Scots, was beheaded on February 8, 1587. Perhaps in remorse, Elizabeth bestowed a pension on Mary's son James, effectively recognizing him as her heir.

International Affairs

The execution of Mary, Queen of Scots, did not stop Catholics from scheming to remove Elizabeth from the throne. Elizabeth's chief Catholic antagonist was King Philip II of Spain. Philip desired to fulfill the papal edict and depose Elizabeth. He was also increasingly frustrated by Elizabeth's "Sea Dogs," privateers who attacked and captured Spanish ships filled with treasures from their conquered territories in the Americas. Men like Sir Francis Drake, Sir John Hawkins, and Sir Walter Raleigh became household names for their adventures at sea. Elizabeth quietly endorsed the Sea Dogs' exploits, especially as the crown retained a portion of the captured booty.

By 1586 Philip had had enough and planned an invasion of England. Assembling the huge Spanish fleet, which history calls the Spanish Armada, took more than a year. Elizabeth was, however, well informed of Spain's intentions and had months to get England ready.

The Spanish Armada

The invasion fleet approached the French coast in late July 1588. On August 9, as the English and Spanish fleets fought in the English Channel, Elizabeth risked her own safety and appeared before her coastal defense troops at Tilbury, where the English believed the Spanish intended to land. Astride a horse, she proclaimed, "Let tyrants fear, I have always so behaved myself that, under God, I have placed my chiefest strength and safeguard in the loyal hearts and good-will of my subjects. . . . I know I have the body but of a weak and feeble woman; but I have the heart and stomach of a king, and of a king of England, too."[26]

The invasion force never set foot on English soil. The Spanish ships were large and heavily armed, but slow and difficult to maneuver. The English ships, including some commanded by the Sea Dogs, were smaller and faster and darted in and out of the armada, attacking and scattering the fleet. Heavy weather at sea aided their efforts, as 44 of the armada's nearly 130 ships were sunk in battle or in storms, and two-thirds of their forty thousand troops perished. The English lost only 1 ship. The defeat of the vaunted Spanish Armada was celebrated as a great victory, and English naval power flourished for centuries to come.

Gloriana

The last fifteen years of Elizabeth's reign marked the height of her power and the high-water mark of a wave of English art and literature. Artists portrayed her as serene and majestic, untouched by the ravages of time. William Shakespeare, Francis Bacon, Edmund Spenser, and others wrote plays and poetry that expounded on England's virtues and the land's rich history, and declared Elizabeth the queen of queens. Shakespeare called her the model for all rulers to follow; Spenser's epic poem *The Faerie*

Thomas Cromwell

Thomas Cromwell, first Earl of Essex, played an important role for ten years during the reign of King Henry VIII. From 1530 to 1540, he was the king's trusted adviser and an advocate of religious reform. He helped bring Henry's "great matter" to a resolution when he convinced the king to break with the Catholic Church. He represented Henry in Parliament, convincing the members to affirm that the king was the leader of a separate Church of England with the power to appoint bishops and archbishops. He also oversaw the confiscation of the Catholic Church's wealth and treasure that enriched Henry's treasury.

Cromwell also played a leading part in the case against Anne Boleyn, collecting evidence and securing confessions (at least one of which came under torture) that led to her execution. Cromwell negotiated the marriage between Henry and Anne of Cleves in 1539, which ended in failure. Cromwell's enemies took advantage of Henry's dissatisfaction and had him arrested on charges of treason and heresy. He was executed on July 28, 1540. The king later stated that he regretted the execution, calling Cromwell the most faithful servant he had ever had.

Thomas Cromwell was Henry VIII's trusted adviser for ten years, but in 1540 Henry had him executed for treason and heresy, which the king later regretted.

Queene was dedicated to her, with the character Gloriana serving as an allegory for the English monarch.

By 1603 only old folks in England could remember any other ruler. Elizabeth's was the longest reign since Edward III's in the 1300s, and at sixty-nine, she was the oldest monarch to have sat on the throne. But she still conducted affairs of state, such as welcoming in Italian a new ambassador from Venice that February. She died peacefully on March 24, 1603, having never officially designated an heir. On her death, her advisers quickly sent a message north to James VI of Scotland. The age of the Tudors was over. The age of the Stuarts was about to begin.

Chapter Four

The Struggle for Power

Upon the death of Elizabeth, James VI, the king of Scotland, wasted no time in leaving his native land to assume his new role as king of England. He headed south in early April 1603 and was in London later that month. He was crowned King James I of England in July. He did not relinquish the Scots crown, however; instead, he would remain James VI in that northern realm.

By the time James Stuart came to the English throne, he had been king of Scotland for more than thirty years. The son of Mary, Queen of Scots, and her second husband, James had been surrounded by political intrigues as he grew up; his first three regents were killed or died before he was six. Consequently, James grew up with a mix of wariness of others and bravado over his survival. But his years of ruling in Scotland had only partially prepared him for his new role.

The First "King of Great Britain"

James I (reigned 1603–1625) was soon challenged by English traditions and methods of government. The Scots Parliament had only one house, populated by hereditary nobles; the English Parliament had the House of Commons, made up of elected untitled men, and the House of Lords, occupied by the nobles. The Scots Parliament had usually followed the king's will without discussion; the English Parliament regularly debated and rejected his proposals. For example, when James I addressed his first session of the English Parliament in March 1604, he proposed uniting the two kingdoms of England and Scotland under the title of "Great Britain." The Scots Parliament approved it; the English Parliament rejected it. While James called himself the king of Great Britain, the two nations continued to have two governments. The new king

King James I dissolved and reconvened Parliament many times, reinstating it when he needed money.

was also uncomfortable with petitioning the House of Commons for various expenditures. Consequently, James "dissolved" Parliament several times during his reign when they refused to do his bidding. The members were dismissed and were no longer involved in state matters until the king recalled them, usually because he needed money.

James's reign was marked by several political successes outside of Parliament, however. Since he was king of both England and Scotland, the cross-border wars that had often occupied both nations came to an end. He succeeded in ending the conflict with Spain, partly by refusing to sanction privateering. He did, however, challenge Spain's dominion over the hemisphere by encouraging English expansion into the New World. During his reign, permanent settlements were

Guy Fawkes and the "Gunpowder Plot"

On the evening of November 5, 1605, a former soldier named Guy Fawkes was discovered in the basement beneath the hall where Parliament was scheduled to open the next day. Nearby was a pile of firewood that hid thirty barrels of gunpowder. He had a pocket watch and matches in his possession and was immediately taken into custody. His arrest led to the discovery of the so-called Gunpowder Plot against King James I and the members of Parliament.

As Fawkes's colleagues were rounded up, the details of the conspiracy came to light. They had planned to blow up the gunpowder to assassinate the king and other members of the government when Parliament opened, and thus spark a Catholic uprising in England. The conspirators then intended to place the king's Catholic daughter Elizabeth on the throne.

Two of Fawkes's coconspirators were killed while resisting arrest; Fawkes and three others were interrogated, tried, and executed for treason. The plot was the work of a small group of extremists, but Catholic persecution intensified in its wake, and citizens were encouraged to light bonfires to celebrate the king's escape. The practice continues in England today every November 5, as bonfires and fireworks mark Guy Fawkes Day.

Guy Fawkes, kneeling, is brought before King James I to be judged. He was hanged for treason, and his plot is commemorated every November 5 in Great Britain, Guy Fawkes Day.

established on the island of Bermuda, at Jamestown (named in his honor and located in present-day Virginia), and at Plymouth (in present-day Massachusetts). He also succeeded in negotiating international alliances with European Protestant leaders through arranged marriages; his most successful was the marriage of his daughter Elizabeth to Frederick, the elector of Palatine (Palatine was an electorate, or state, of the Holy Roman Empire in what is now Germany). He also was a leading proponent among European monarchs of the "divine right of kings," the belief that because kings were chosen to rule by God, kings were only answerable to God (in other words, not subject to the dictates of other men). But he is perhaps most remembered for his translation and adaptation of the Bible into what has become known as the "King James Version," which was published in 1611.

Running both kingdoms took its toll on James; by the middle of the decade 1610–1620, he was showing signs of premature senility. His elder son, Henry, the Prince of Wales, died in 1612, making his younger son Charles the heir apparent. Before he died on March 17, 1625, James warned Charles about the growing power of Parliament and the dangers that awaited Charles as king. Charles failed to heed the advice.

Charles I (reigned 1625–1649)

Charles I had a troubled childhood. He had a weak constitution and did not learn how to talk until he was four years old or how to walk until he was seven. Although he grew into a handsome adult, he was relatively short at five feet four and never lost his childhood stutter. These characteristics, however, did not prevent him from being king. In fact, he believed, as his father had, that he had been chosen by God to be king and did not recognize any earthly authority over his command. This attitude got him into trouble throughout his reign.

During his first three years on the throne, Charles found himself at war, first with Spain and then with France, due in large part to the adventurism of the Duke of Buckingham. Buckingham, who had been a close friend and adviser to James I, continued under Charles to mount ill-advised and expensive military campaigns that resulted in English defeats. Each led Charles to petition Parliament for more money, and like his father, he discovered that Parliament often rebuffed him, in large part because Buckingham was unpopular. Buckingham's assassination in 1628 did not improve Charles's relations with Parliament. Instead, Charles became increasingly influenced by his French Catholic wife, Henrietta, rather than his Protestant advisers. He continued to demand more revenue and refused to listen to opinions different from his own. Out of frustration with the squabbles with Parliament and convinced that he was chosen by God to be king, Charles dismissed Parliament in March 1629 and ruled without it for the next decade.

Cavaliers and Roundheads

When Charles finally did call a new Parliament in April 1639, the old animosities had not disappeared. They had festered and were accompanied by new ones. Charles had been trying to impose Church of England standards on the Scots church to ensure uniformity of worship in his kingdom. The Scots objected, and Charles tried to enforce his policy by force, only to suffer a humiliating defeat. At the same time, an offshoot of Protestantism called Puritanism was gaining followers throughout the kingdom. Puritans advocated a strict interpretation of the Bible and severe restrictions on dress and behavior. The new Parliament, which included many Puritans, refused to finance an additional military campaign, and so the king dismissed it after just a few weeks. The following year, the pattern was repeated, except that this time, the leaders of Parliament forced the king to agree to hear

Charles I is tried for treason. Charles believed that the only authority was that of the divine right of kings and refused to recognize that the court had authority over him. He was beheaded on January 30, 1649.

their grievances and to agree not to dissolve the body in return for considering his funding request. This session became known as the Long Parliament.

By January 1642, however, Charles had tired of Parliament's endless demands for civil reform and tax relief, and he tried to have the leaders of the opposition arrested in their meeting halls. But the men had already escaped, and Charles realized too late that he had gone too far. He fled London to try to rally support for his cause. Seven months of negotiations to avoid open hostilities resulted in nothing as neither side budged from its position. Finally, in August 1642, Charles declared war on the opposition.

Those who supported the king in the war that followed were called Royalists or Cavaliers. The Parliamentarians were called Roundheads, after the shape of the helmets they wore. The Cavaliers carried the early engagements, but the Roundheads' New Model Army under Thomas Fairfax and Oliver Cromwell achieved important victories at Marston Moor in 1644 and at Naseby in 1645. After his defeat at Naseby, Charles was truly on the defensive. He sought refuge in Scotland but was handed over to Fairfax and Cromwell, who tried to get him to agree to a written constitution. He escaped their custody, fled to Scotland again, raised an army, and was finally and decisively defeated in August 1648.

The Roundheads' leaders insisted that the king be put on trial for waging war against his people. The Commons convened a court of justice in January 1649.

Charles, a lifelong believer in the divine right of kings, proclaimed that a king could do no wrong and refused to recognize that the court had authority over him. Consequently, he offered no arguments in his defense. By a one-vote margin, the court condemned him to death on January 27, 1649. On the execution scaffold three days later, he proclaimed that he had desired the liberty and freedom of the people as much as anyone else but added, "I must tell you that the liberty and freedom [of the people] consists in having a government.... It is not for having a share in government.... A subject and a sovereign are clear[ly] different things."[27]

With one stroke of the axe, the reign of Charles I was over. He was forty-eight years old. The Parliamentarians had killed the king; now the challenge was to run the nation without one.

The Commonwealth (1649–1661)

The conflict between the Royalists and the Parliamentarians is known in British history as the Civil War. As Mike Ashley puts it, "This was not the first civil war to divide England, and it was not the first to result in the deposition of a king, but because it was the first and only war to result in the abolition of the kingship, it has become known as *the* Civil War."[28] Parliament quickly abolished the House of Lords for its support of the king, leaving only the House of Commons. The body, known as the Rump Parliament, then passed a law forbidding anyone from proclaiming another king. Instead,

Oliver Cromwell dissolved Parliament in April 1653 after becoming Lord Protector. For the next six years he would rule as if he were king.

the leadership of the new republic, which was called the Commonwealth, fell to Oliver Cromwell.

Cromwell had been a member of Parliament since 1628, and as leader of the victorious Roundheads, he seemed to be the best choice for building a bridge between the army and Parliament. Following the king's execution, Cromwell returned to Parliament and was selected to serve on the Council of State, which worked with Parliament to run England. But his time at Parliament was short-lived, as he and his army were dispatched to quell an uprising of Catholics and Royalists in Ireland. His nine-month campaign there led to widespread car-

nage and deportations of Irish rebels to English colonies in America. He then left for Scotland to deal with a similar rebellion, where Royalists had named the late king's son, Charles Stuart, King Charles II.

By 1652 the rebellions had been defeated, and Stuart was in exile in Europe. Cromwell returned to Parliament, and in 1653 he accused it of refusing to move forward with elections and reforms and dissolved it with the help of his army. The following year, he was sworn in as Lord Protector under a new government framework. The position was his for life.

For the next six years, Cromwell ruled much as previous kings had. He

The Act of Habeas Corpus

In 1679 the English Parliament passed landmark legislation that reverberates through legal systems to this day. The Act of Habeas Corpus codified the right of a prisoner, or a prisoner's representative, to petition for immediate release under suspicion of unlawful imprisonment. The term *habeas corpus*, meaning "you have the body," comes from the original Latin of the court order, or writ, allowing the imprisoned to be released.

Under the act, a petitioner presents an appeal to a judge, who then issues a writ, or order, of habeas corpus, which compels the authority imprisoning the petitioner to release him or her until the legality of the imprisonment can be determined. The right of habeas corpus had existed in England since at least the fourteenth century, and perhaps even predated the rights established under the Magna Carta in 1215. The 1679 act officially put that right into law.

Since 1679 habeas corpus has been incorporated into national constitutions around the world. According to Michael Zander, professor emeritus of law at the London School of Economics, habeas corpus "represents the fundamental principle that unlawful detention can be challenged by immediate access to a judge—even by telephone in the middle of the night."

Quoted in BBC News. "A Brief History of Habeas Corpus." March 9, 2005. http://news.bbc.co.uk/2/hi/uk _news/magazine/4329839.stm.

called Parliaments only when he wanted money for wars. He first went to war with Holland over merchant trading rights and then allied with France against Spain over control of Flanders (part of modern Belgium). He tried to impose his brand of religion on the land, but his form of Puritan Protestantism was too stark and pessimistic for many Britons. Cromwell designated his son as his successor. He died from blood poisoning, likely connected to kidney stones, on September 3, 1658. His son's brief time as Lord Protector was highly ineffective,

and by 1660 there was a groundswell for the restoration of the monarchy. From exile in Holland, Charles Stuart sent a letter to Parliament promising goodwill, pardons, and freedom of religion. Parliament sent a ship to bring him home, and Stuart returned to England on May 26, 1660. He was crowned Charles II the following April. The Commonwealth was no more.

The Restoration

For many in England, the return of the monarchy, called the Restoration, was like a breath of fresh air. A newly elected Parliament rolled back many of the reforms instituted during the Commonwealth, such as the bans on many public celebrations and feast days. The new king was an amusing and likeable man with a great sense of humor, who inspired a rebirth of the arts and sciences through his participation in many activities that Cromwell's Puritans had forbidden. Charles (reigned 1661–1685) not only lifted the Puritan ban on theater performances but regularly supported and patronized performances throughout London. He enjoyed horse racing and sailing. He established the Royal Society in 1660 to expand scientific investigation of the natural world and lent support to the Royal Observatory to expand investigation of the heavens.

An underlying current of religious intolerance, however, remained from the Commonwealth. Each subsequent election sent more Puritans to Parliament, and various laws banning minority faiths troubled the king. He had developed Catholic tendencies during his years in exile (in part due to his Catholic mother, the former queen), and he married Catherine of Braganza, a Portuguese Catholic, in 1662. His brother James, the Duke of York, was openly Catholic. Suspicions of the king's true sympathies increased when he issued his Declaration of Indulgence in 1672, which allowed private worship for Catholics and suspended all penalties for nonconformity with the English church. The backlash against Catholics continued to rise.

This backlash was manifested in a variety of rumors of Catholic plots against the government, the Church of England, and against the king. Rumors arose that Catholics had been responsible for starting London's Great Fire of 1666, which burned over thirteen thousand homes and nearly one hundred churches. In 1678 a former Jesuit named Titus Oates spread stories of the so-called Popish Plot, in which Irish Catholics were said to be set to invade England, overthrow the king, and place his Catholic brother on the throne. The investigation took two years to reveal that the story was a hoax, but in that time, over thirty-five Catholics were tried and executed, including the Duke of York's former private secretary. The so-called Rye-House Plot of 1683 was a plan formed by some of the king's opponents to assassinate both Charles and James, and to put the king's eldest, and illegitimate, son on the throne. When the king and his supporters discovered the plot, they ordered the executions of many who were involved in it.

After the Rye-House Plot, agitation diminished, and Charles's reign was peaceful. He did not live long thereafter, however, as he suffered a stroke and died on February 6, 1685, at age fifty-four. He and his wife had no children, so the throne passed to his brother James.

The Glorious Revolution

On Charles's deathbed, he had been received into the Catholic Church. His brother, now James II (reigned 1685–1688), was already openly Catholic and, after the death of his first wife, had married an Italian Catholic. Suspicions arose that England was heading toward rejoining the Catholic Church and undoing all the work of Henry VIII. To many Protestants and a large number of members of Parliament, this was unacceptable. Their hopes for a continued Protestant England lay in James's daughters, both of whom were Protestants. Mary had married William of Orange, one of the leading Protestants in Holland, and Anne had married George, the brother of the king of Protestant Denmark. They believed that because James and his second wife had had no surviving children, upon his death, the throne would pass to Mary. But in the summer of 1688, after fifteen years of delivering children that were either stillborn or did not survive infancy, James's wife gave birth to a healthy son.

On June 30, 1688, the bishop of London and six supporters wrote to William of Orange, inviting him to England to take over the government. They assured him, "There are nineteen parts of twenty of the people throughout the kingdom who are desirous of a change"[29] and hoped that he would protect his wife's claim to the throne. William agreed, and in November he landed with an army in southwestern England. James's support vanished as both the army and the navy threw their support to William. James's daughter Anne abandoned him as well. In December James fled from London, and William accepted the reins of government on December 29, 1688. The following year a member of Parliament described the events as a "Glorious Revolution," the name by which it is still known today.

History has remembered James II as impatient and arrogant, but at the same time, in the words of historian Maurice Ashley, because he was "conscious of his father's fate on the scaffold, he surrendered his throne too easily to his son-in-law."[30] He lived on in exile in France at the court of his friend King Louis XIV, where he died in 1701.

William (reigned 1689–1702) and Mary (reigned 1689–1694)

When Parliament met in early 1689, they declared that James had abdicated by deserting the country, which cleared the way for Mary to become queen. Mary, however, was uncomfortable being the sole ruler as it might appear that she had usurped her father's throne, and William, for his part, did not want to be a king consort. A series of negotiations resulted in Parliament offering William and Mary joint sovereignty. In other words, they would rule equally and one would continue to rule if the other died.

Before they were offered the crown, William and Mary were asked to agree to a number of resolutions called the Declaration of Right. The declaration limited the sovereign's power, reaffirmed Parliament's right to tax and legislate, required the sovereign to call Parliament frequently, and dictated that the sovereign affirm the Protestant faith in the coronation speech. It further excluded James II, his heirs, and all Catholics from the throne,

As a result of negotiations with Parliament, William and Mary ruled jointly, but Parliament reaffirmed its right to tax and legislate.

since "it hath been found by experience that it is inconsistent with the safety and welfare of this protestant kingdom to be governed by a papist prince."[31] Following their acceptance of the declaration, the husband and wife were crowned William III and Mary II on April 11, 1689.

The declaration was just the first new limitation enacted under their reign and was due to the still-fresh memories of Charles I, the Long Parliament, and the Commonwealth. Other acts included a measure that required the monarch to call for Parliamentary elections at

The Acts of Union, 1707

In the early 1700s, both King William III and Queen Anne proposed that the kingdoms of England and Scotland be formally unified. The Scots objected, mostly due to the 1701 Act of Succession. The Scots wanted the freedom to choose their own monarch when Anne died. The English Parliament forced the matter in 1705 when it passed the Aliens Act, which, if enforced, would have treated Scots as foreigners and prohibited trade with Scotland. The Scots eventually accepted the Hanoverian succession, and negotiations led to the Acts of Union passed by each Parliament.

Under the Acts, Scotland and England united as "Great Britain." The act called for a common coinage and a common flag, reformed land taxes in Scotland, and gave Scotland economic equality with England. Additionally, the Scots Parliament would be abolished in favor of Scots representation in a new British Parliament. Both parties agreed to the terms, and on May 1, 1707, the union of the two kingdoms became official and the Kingdom of Great Britain was born.

least every three years and an act that prohibited funding a standing army in peacetime, except by permission of the Commons. Each of these contributed to the formation of Great Britain's constitutional monarchy, in which the sovereign remains the head of the nation, but the power over day-to-day affairs and to make laws lies in the Parliament.

As it turned out, William was less interested in the day-to-day affairs of kingship than he was in using England as a base for military campaigns. He spent the spring and summer of nearly every year overseas in one battle or another. For example, he defeated a combined French and Irish force dedicated to James II at the Battle of the Boyne in Ireland on July 1, 1690; from 1692 to 1695 he fought several campaigns in Europe as part of an alliance of nations against France's Louis XIV. During these absences, Mary presided over the government and proved an able administrator.

The Succession Crisis

The partnership under which William and Mary had governed changed when Mary contracted smallpox and died in December 1694. She was just thirty-three. Shortly before her death, William wrote to a friend, "You can imagine what a state I am in, loving her as I do. You know what it is to have a good wife."[32] Gilbert Burnet, the bishop of Salisbury, wrote that when Mary died, William's "spirits sunk so low that there was great reason to apprehend that he was following her."[33] They had had no children, and William never remarried. When Mary's sister Anne's surviving son, the eleven-year-old William, Duke of Gloucester, died in 1700, there were no more direct heirs to the throne. His death prompted a succession crisis.

The challenge was to find and designate an heir who fit the hereditary and Parliamentary requirements. In 1701 Parliament passed the Act of Succession, which bypassed the Catholic heirs in favor of Princess Sophia, electress of Hanover. She was the daughter of the queen of Bohemia and a granddaughter of James I. At the time, she was already seventy, so it seemed unlikely that she would live to rule in England. But her son was forty, and her grandson was seventeen. The act seemed to settle the dynastic question.

William died in 1702 following a horse riding accident in which he fell and broke his collarbone. During his convalescence, pneumonia set in, and the lifelong asthmatic died on March 8, 1702. His sister-in-law Anne, the last of the Protestant Stuarts, ascended the throne at the age of thirty-seven.

Anne (reigned 1702–1714)

By the time Anne became queen in 1702, she had been married to Prince George of Denmark for almost twenty years. During that time, Anne had been pregnant eighteen times, giving birth to only one healthy child. Of the remaining children, fourteen, including a set of twins, were stillborn. As Mike Ashley observes,

"Since each child arrived within scarcely a year of the previous one, Anne's body must have been exhausted."[34] That she kept her general good humor and kindhearted generosity is a tribute to her character. For example, she was a staunch advocate of the Church of England and used her own private resources to establish a fund known as Queen Anne's Bounty to augment the pay of poorer clergy.

Anne's dozen years as queen were dominated by the War of the Spanish Succession, which was prompted when the French king, Louis XIV, accepted the throne of Spain on behalf of his grandson. This violated an international treaty from 1700 that designated Charles of Austria as the rightful heir. Louis's actions would have united France and Spain, two of Europe's most powerful nations, under one rule. Nations chose their allies based on their support or their opposition to Louis's actions. Britain, opposed to the unification, was allied with Austria, Portugal, Denmark, and the Netherlands against France, Spain, and Bavaria. The war resulted in several successes for Britain, including the 1704 seizure from Spain of Gibraltar (which continues as a British territory to this day) and the much-celebrated victory of John Churchill, the Duke of Marlborough, against the French army at the Battle of Blenheim that same year.

The war, however, dragged on year after year, draining Britain's resources and straining the people's patience before it ground to a close in 1713. Anne's popularity among the people remained high, but she had several quarrels with politicians and, perhaps most famously, with Marlborough's wife, Sarah. Sarah, who had been an assistant to Anne since before Anne was queen, championed her husband's cause, insisting that Anne bestow upon them and their family a never-ending list of rewards. After Anne's husband, George, died in 1708, she appeared moody and depressed but still played a role in the government by dismissing advisers and ministers who she believed did not have the nation's best interests at heart. She also dismissed Marlborough and his wife for neglecting their official duties, though it pained her to do so.

By the end of 1713, her health was failing. In June 1714 the electress Sophia died, making her son George Ludwig the heir apparent. Anne suffered a stroke six weeks later on July 30, 1714, and died on August 1. Her doctor, John Arbuthnot, wrote, "I believe sleep was never more welcome to a weary traveler than death was to her."[35] She was the last of the Stuart monarchs.

Chapter Five

The Hanoverian Succession

With the death of Queen Anne in August 1714, the Act of Succession went into effect. In the words of John Cannon and Ralph Griffiths, "Everything pointed to a desperate race for the throne" between George Ludwig, elector of Hanover, and James II's son James Francis Edward Stuart, who lived in France. Instead it was, according to Cannon and Griffiths, "one of the grand anti-climaxes of British history."[36] Stuart made no effort to assert his claim, even as George made a leisurely trip of six weeks from Hanover to England.

George Ludwig was crowned King George I on October 20, 1714. At age fifty-four, he was older than any previous British heir had been upon taking the throne. His ascension was not met with universal acclaim; in fact, he was jeered as he paraded through the streets of London after his coronation. By this time, according to Mike Ashley, "the power of the king was waning against the growing power of Parliament and, while the authority of the king retained a certain mystical aura, this was not what it had been before the Civil War and the English were already starting to regard the monarch as a figurehead."[37] Others disliked him in the same way they had disliked William III: He was a foreigner. Yet his reign began a more than one-hundred-year-long succession of Hanoverian kings ruling Britain.

George I (reigned 1714–1727)

By the time he became king of Great Britain, George had already had an adventurous life. His marriage had ended in divorce in 1694 when his wife had an affair with an army officer. He imprisoned her for the rest of her life; her lover mysteriously disappeared, and George was suspected of having ordered his murder. George became the elector, or ruler, of Hanover in 1698, worked with English officers during the War of the Spanish Succession, and commanded an army from 1707 to 1709. He was fit and athletic into middle age before becoming quite large in his later years. When he came to England, his two mistresses accompanied him; one was so thin that she soon acquired the nickname the Maypole; the other was so stout that when she and the king were seen together, they were called Elephant and Castle.

George I was well educated and had an avid interest in science. He created the Royal Academy of Music in 1720.

George was well educated and took an interest in a number of scientific pursuits such as the latest agricultural advancements. He particularly enjoyed music, including the work of composer George Frideric Handel. In fact, Handel composed his widely celebrated *Water Music* for one of the king's parties in 1715. The king's love of Handel's work led to the creation of the first Royal Academy of Music in 1720. The king's first language was German, and while he struggled with English, he had a good command of French, the diplomatic language of the era.

His relations with his son George Augustus, the Prince of Wales, however, were strained no matter which language they used. The prince had a better command of English and often translated for his father in cabinet meetings. They had a falling-out in 1717 when they had an argument at the baptism of the prince's new son. Consequently, the prince stayed away from future cabinet meetings and assembled a group of his own advisers from the government, including Robert Walpole, the leader of the majority Whig Party in Parliament. The dispute with his son forced George to find someone else to represent him at the cabinet meetings and to provide direction for the government. Today, this post is known as the prime minister.

Although the title did not yet exist, some historians consider Walpole Britain's first prime minister. George did not like Walpole, but the king in his later years grudgingly relied on the skill of Walpole, who proved instrumental in helping rescue the nation's economy from disaster and the government from scandal in 1720. For several years, Britons from all walks of life, including the royal family and government officials, had been purchasing stock in a firm called the South Sea Company. As more and more stock sold, driving the price higher and higher, the owners started promising dividends they could not deliver. In the spring of 1720, the stock's price increased by almost 800 percent before plunging over the summer as investors tried to cash in. When the company went bankrupt, due in part to some shady activities by cabinet members and government ministers, thousands of people lost everything. In the aftermath, Walpole succeeded in restoring confidence in the government by revamping treasury practices and pushing through reforming legislation.

Like Father, Like Son

George I's later years had fewer upheavals. He liked to spend his summers in Hanover, and on a trip there in June 1727, he died from a cerebral hemorrhage and was succeeded by George Augustus without any protests at home or abroad. The forty-four-year-old became George II (reigned 1727–1760). After the Act of Succession had put him in line to the throne, he had been tutored in English and the English way of life. In his later years he spoke about being more English than German, even if, according to Mike Ashley, "he said it in a strong German accent."[38]

Despite their differences, George II was like his father in some ways. He treated his son, Frederick, the Prince of Wales, much as he had been treated. Frederick, who was twenty when his father became George II, soon became a dashing figure in London society and a thorn in his parents' sides. The king said Frederick's popularity made him nauseous; George's wife, Queen Caroline, called Frederick "that wretch" and "that villain."[39] Perhaps their anger was because Frederick amassed large gambling debts that his parents refused to pay or perhaps it was that Frederick cultivated relationships with his father's political opponents. In any case, by the time Frederick died of an aneurysm in 1751 at age forty-four, he had married and fathered nine children, which removed the king's younger (and favorite) son from the succession.

George II's popularity among his people had grown as the nation prospered. A contributing factor in the prosperity was Britain's colonial empire in North America, which provided a ready market for British goods and was a source of seemingly unlimited raw materials. But as was the case with many of his predecessors, George became embroiled in European politics. The War of the Austrian Succession began in 1739, and soon Britain was at war with both Spain and France. The king, nearly sixty now, led an army of British, Austrian, Dutch, Hanoverian, and Hessian troops against the French at the Battle of Dettingen in June 1743. He rallied the troops under heavy fire, saying, "Now boys! Now for the honor of England! Fire and behave brave, and the French will run."[40] The allied victory marked the last time a British king led troops into battle. Britain also went to war with France in the Seven Years' War in 1756, which resulted in territorial gains in Canada, India, the West Indies, and Africa.

By this time, George was in his mid-seventies. During his reign, the British Empire had grown considerably, and the nation was flourishing. His declining health, however, led to increasing bouts of constipation, and on the morning of October 25, 1760, he suffered a fatal heart attack while sitting on the toilet.

George III (reigned 1760–1820)

Frederick's son George assumed the throne upon the death of George II. He was the first king from the House of Hanover to be born in England. In some ways, he could be as stubborn as his grandfather, but he learned the value of being flexible and open to change. He delayed his coronation until after his marriage to Charlotte of Mecklenburg-Strelitz in September 1761 so they could have a joint ceremony as king and queen. They had an extremely long and prosperous marriage, resulting in the birth of fifteen children.

One of the king's top priorities was bringing an end to the war with France and Spain. The Treaty of Paris in 1763 brought an end to the fighting, but it had been a long and expensive war. The British had been involved in battles from Canada to India and were now hard pressed

Jonathan Swift's
Gulliver's Travels

In 1726 a two-volume work titled *Travels into Several Remote Nations of the World, in Four Parts. By Lemuel Gulliver, First a Surgeon, and Then a Captain of Several Ships* appeared in London. The tales, now usually called *Gulliver's Travels*, were written by Jonathan Swift, and consisted of a fascinating collection of stories of adventure, discovery, and hardship.

Swift's tales recount the fanciful explorations of unknown lands, where by turns the normal-sized Gulliver towers over the miniature inhabitants of Lilliput and then is a miniature plaything to the giants of Brobdingnag. Gulliver's remarks about the people and places he visited were first full of optimism at the outward appearances of well-being and harmony, but were then followed by observations of their darker sides, including intolerance, ignorance, and war.

The readers of eighteenth-century London, however, understood that the tales were much more than just fiction. Swift lampooned the way kings and queens related to their people and their neighbors, the way governments worked, and the undercurrent of religious intolerance based on differing beliefs. The work remains both a fantastic narrative of imaginary places and an important satire of eighteenth-century English culture.

to pay for them. Following the war's end, Parliament tried to raise revenue through a number of taxes on everyday items and publications. These efforts had mixed results; one, the Stamp Act of 1765, was so unpopular that it was repealed a year later. The taxes were also unpopular in Britain's colonies, especially in America. The American colonies had no representation in Parliament, and many colonists believed they were being taxed by a government without their approval. Negotiations between colonial and government representatives for taxation reform failed, and by 1775 the American colonies were in open rebellion.

Troubled Times

At first George had no intention of letting the colonies leave the empire. His prime minister, Lord North, worked to put down the insurrection, but the war, now known as the American Revolution, dragged on for several years, straining the British treasury. French and Spanish aid assisted the American cause, leading to a series of stunning colonial victories and Lord Cornwallis's surrender of the British army at Yorktown in 1781. Lord North became resigned to the fact that the Americans had won their independence. After two years of negotiations, the two sides agreed to the Treaty of

Paris in 1783, which recognized American independence.

For a king to lose colonies to another monarch was one thing; to grant them independence was another. Rulers were accustomed to succeeding at quashing rebellions, no matter the cost. Catherine the Great, the empress of Russia, was shocked at this outcome, saying, "Rather than have granted America her Independence as my brother monarch King George has done, I would have fired a

King George III would bring an end to the Seven Years' War but would lose the American colonies to independence.

George III's "Madness"

By the year 1800 King George III's periodic bouts of violence, hyperactivity, and mental imbalance were well known across Great Britain. The king suffered from these attacks throughout his adult life, sometimes lasting weeks or months. The final bout lasted almost nine years.

Nineteenth-century medicine considered his affliction "madness," or insanity (in other words, a mental illness). Modern medical practitioners have tried to understand the king's condition based on reviews of the observations made by his doctors and by those around him. Early twentieth-century researchers theorized that George's condition was the result of a manic-depressive psychosis, and some twenty-first-century investigators have combined current mental health understanding and historical research to lend weight to this theory.

An additional theory suggests that George suffered from an inherited blood disease called *porphyria*. The disease's symptoms include abdominal pain, rapid heart rate, hallucinations, depression, and paranoia. During an attack of porphyria, the patient's urine is discolored a deep blue or purple, giving the disease its name (from the Greek word for "purple"). Each of these symptoms was observed by George's doctors. The theory received widespread attention in the wake of the 1994 film *The Madness of King George*, which included in the credits a statement linking the king's condition to porphyria.

pistol at my own head."[41] But George had come to the realization that American independence was best for all. When he met with the United States ambassador, John Adams, in 1785, the king said, "I will be free with you. I was the last to consent to the separation; but the separation having been made and having become inevitable, I have always said, as I say now, that I would be the first to meet the friendship of the United States as an independent power."[42]

While the government's reputation suffered tremendously due to the loss of the American colonies, George remained personally popular among the people. They did not hold him responsible for the hard times that marked the end of the eighteenth century. Most of the population's complaints, according to Mike Ashley, were "aimed at the government and not directly at George. . . . In fact he was often viewed, especially by the middle classes, as their champion against the government."[43]

The protests, called the Gordon Riots of 1780, were a dispute against the government and a reaction to Parliament's attempts to ease laws discriminating against Catholics. Under the instigation of Lord George Gordon, a member of Parliament and president of the Anti-Catholic Protestant Association, mobs rioted in London for a week in June. On June 2, 1780, a mob assembled near Parliament. An eyewitness named Ignatius Sancho described the scene: "There is at this present moment at least a hundred thousand poor, miserable, ragged rabble, from twelve to sixty years of age . . . —besides half as many women and children—all parading the streets—the bridge—the park—ready for any and every mischief."[44]

The mob assaulted members of Parliament in the streets, burned homes, and freed prisoners from two jails before they tore them down. The riots continued for a week as ministers and members of Parliament fled London. King George, however, refused to leave, and ordered the army to disperse the protesters by firing into the crowd. Over two hundred died in the melee that followed, but peace was restored. While George was later the target of two assassination attempts, one in 1786 and another in 1800, both assailants were declared insane, and George remained as popular as ever.

This domestic turmoil was mirrored by Britain's involvement in the Napoleonic Wars. Following the upheavals of the French Revolution of 1789, the French king and queen were beheaded and the monarchy abolished. French military leader Napoléon Bonaparte seized power in 1799 and soon sought to overrun the continent. The British navy defeated Bonaparte's fleet in 1805 at Trafalgar, and after ten more years of devastating warfare throughout Europe, the British army and its allies defeated the French at Waterloo in 1815. The victories restored the public's confidence in Britain's martial might after the loss of the American colonies. This confidence was, however, offset by concern about the king himself.

The King's "Madness"

In 1765 George suffered the first bout of what seemed to be a type of insanity. He talked incessantly, or not at all, failed to recognize family members, and acted irrationally and occasionally violently. This attack may have been brought on by the strains of government, but it was merely a taste of things to come. By the time he had a second bout in 1788, his children were mostly grown and his son George, the Prince of Wales, sought to be declared regent over his father. But the king began to recover, and the proposal was set aside. He had further attacks in 1801 and 1804, and when his youngest daughter, Amelia, died in November 1810, George descended into another bout from which he did not emerge. The prince was declared regent in 1811.

By then, the king was blind and was confined to Windsor Castle, where he roamed the halls in a violet dressing gown, unkempt and neglected. He declared he could converse with the dead. He talked about plans to escape to Denmark. He pounded out discordant melodies on a harpsichord. His doctors announced that "he appears to be living in another world, and has lost almost all interest in the concern of this."[45] He finally died on January 29, 1820, at age eighty-one. He had ruled through an especially turbulent time in history, which had seen the loss of the American colonies, the end of the French monarchy, the rise and fall of Napoléon, and challenging economic times; yet, under his leadership, the nation had triumphed abroad against Napoléon's aggression and had advanced socially important measures, such as the abolition of the slave trade. His son, the prince regent, now became king.

George IV (reigned 1820–1830)

When George III died after almost sixty years on the throne, the Prince of Wales had been king in almost every sense of the word, but without the title, for close to ten years. Because of his father's long reign, he was forty-eight when he became regent. By then, he had been the subject of a number of embarrassing incidents that had caused his parents great pain. He was a spoiled child who grew up to have several mistresses and illegitimate children before falling in love with a twice-widowed woman named Mary Fitzherbert. The prince knew the king would never approve of the match, as Fitzherbert was a commoner and a Catholic, but they were married in a secret ceremony in December 1785. When this was revealed, the king was furious and refused to sanction the marriage, and the two were quickly and quietly divorced.

At the king's insistence, the prince married Princess Caroline of Brunswick (in the German lands of the Holy Roman Empire) in April 1795, but they soon discovered they were ill suited for each other. They had a daughter, Charlotte, nine months later, but separated soon after that. The prince returned to his mistresses. Charlotte died in 1817 from complications in childbirth, leaving the prince regent without an heir. Caroline,

King George IV insisted on marrying Princess Caroline of Brunswick, but they soon found out they were incompatible.

who had been on a European tour when George III died, returned to England despite the new king's attempts to pay her to stay away. She was not crowned queen at his coronation, and died in 1821.

With the ceremony, his days as regent officially came to a close. The periods both before and after the coronation, however, are known as The Regency and were marked by extravagance in architecture, parties, fashion, and the arts. The king oversaw the massive reconstructions of Windsor Castle and Buckingham Palace and supported a rebuilding of a portion of central London into a new park and neighborhood now called The Regent's Park. The Regency also marked the dawn of the Industrial Revolution in Britain. Advancements in agriculture meant landowners needed fewer workers in the fields; many of these displaced workers migrated to the cities, hoping to find jobs. But at the same time, advancements in mechanization led to the development of machines that could spin wool, weave cloth, and perform other tasks that had previously been done by hand. While manufacturers profited, workers suffered, and protests by both rural and urban populations grew loud by the 1820s.

The last few years of his reign found George IV in seclusion at Windsor Castle. Politics had never been his strong suit; now he removed himself from the nation's business altogether. Surrounded by several of his earlier mistresses, he lived out his final days and died on June 26, 1830, at age sixty-seven. He left no direct heirs, and the crown passed to his younger brother William, the Duke of Clarence.

William IV (reigned 1830–1837)

William had not expected to be king. He was the third son of George III and Queen Charlotte, but circumstances beyond his control threw him into the succession. First, the Prince of Wales's only child, his daughter Charlotte, died in 1817. Then, William's older brother Frederick (George III's second son) died without children in 1827. Only then did it become apparent that William was the heir to the throne.

By that time, William had spent his entire adult life in the British navy. He joined in 1779 as a low-ranking sailor before moving up the ranks. In 1788 he was given command of his first ship, and in 1789 he was made a rear admiral and named the Duke of Clarence. He retired from the navy in 1790, and in the same year began a relationship with an actress named Dorothea Bland, who used the stage name "Mrs. Jordan." Over the next several years, they had ten children together, all of whom took the last name of Fitzclarence (the prefix "Fitz" comes from the French word *fils*, or "son of"). Bland died in 1816, but because the children born to her and William were illegitimate, none of them were in line for the throne.

When the prince regent's daughter died in 1817, both William and his brother Frederick sought legitimate marriages to continue the family line. In 1818 William married Adelaide, the

William IV was an accomplished naval officer, but as king he repeatedly was at odds with Parliament. He was not in favor of reforms but believed they were in the best interest of the nation.

eldest daughter of the German Duke of Saxe-Coburg-Meiningen. William was fifty-two; she was twenty-five. Despite the age difference, they were devoted to each other, and Adelaide made a fine stepmother to the Fitzclarence children. None of their own children, however, survived infancy.

"Who Is Silly Billy Now?"

William's reputation was not good. His family had nicknamed him Silly Billy because he seemed a likeable fool. In the navy he had developed a taste for expressing his opinion forthrightly with sometimes salty language and a reputation for taking action when he saw the

The Luddites

A s the Industrial Revolution spread throughout Great Britain, many who were affected by the societal changes of increased mechanization began to voice their objections. One group was called the Luddites. The group took its name from a character named Ned Ludd who supposedly lived in Sherwood Forest, the home of the mythical Robin Hood. The Luddites protested mechanization by destroying industrial machines developed for the textile industries in north-central England. According to British historian Marjie Bloy, "There does not seem to have been any political motivation behind the Luddite riots; equally, there was no national organization. The men merely were attacking what they saw as the reason for the decline in their livelihoods."

In April 1812 Luddites attacked two mills, assaulting one owner and killing the other. Trials and Parliamentary investigations followed. Three men were hanged for the murder. Additional trials and executions followed an outbreak in 1816 in which Luddites destroyed over fifty machines before troops were used to end the riots. From that point, Luddite activity faded away.

Today, the term *luddite* is often applied to two types of individuals: those who do not understand the latest technological advances, and those who deliberately avoid them.

Marjie Bloy. "The Luddites, 1811–1816." The Victorian Web, December 30, 2005. www.victorianweb.org /history/riots/luddites.html.

---

need. When it became apparent that he was next in line for the throne, he took great care to maintain his health, and when George IV's servant announced the king's death, William could scarcely contain his glee. When he received the allegiances of the members of the Privy Council, he exclaimed, "Who is Silly Billy now?"[46]

From the beginning, he took his role extremely seriously. There was a backlog of thousands of documents that his brother had ignored; he stayed up far into the night to sign his name to them. He refused to have an extravagant coronation and proclaimed that his would cost a tenth of what his brother's ceremony had cost, which made him popular among his subjects.

He was not, however, a skilled politician, and he butted heads with the leaders of Parliament over a variety of issues. He locked horns with members of the House of Lords in 1832 over legislation designed to reform the House of Commons' election process, which was outdated and subject to abuse. The king personally was not in favor of the reform, and the majority of the lords were against it also. But William realized that it was in the nation's best interest and convinced the lords not to vote against it. Additional social legislation regulated child labor and abolished slavery in British colonies.

But at the heart of William's reign was his feeling that he was merely a caretaker. His heir apparent was the daughter of his younger brother, the Duke of Kent, who had died in 1820. The duke's daughter, named Victoria, had been born in 1819 and never knew her father. The king and Victoria's mother, the duchess, however, never got along, and he was determined to live long enough for Victoria to turn eighteen, so that she would be old enough to rule without her mother as regent. He got his wish; when he died of pneumonia and cirrhosis of the liver on June 20, 1837, Victoria was one month past her eighteenth birthday.

The Last of the Hanoverian Kings

William IV had understood his role within the developing constitutional monarchy well. The monarchy had evolved from the years when the king's word was law to an age when the ruler merely advised. William summed up this change when he said, "I have my view of things, and I tell them to my ministers. If they do not adopt them, I cannot help it. I have done my duty."[47]

By the time William died, the population of Great Britain had grown to 25 million, and 2 million of those lived in London. The Industrial Revolution had led to the growth of other cities, including Liverpool, Manchester, and Glasgow. The new transportation phenomenon of railroads was growing quickly, and iron steamships were beginning to replace wooden sailing vessels on the high seas. William was the last of the Hanoverian kings, and the succession crises that seemed to occur every time a British monarch died now belonged to a bygone era. In fact, the monarchy, and the public perception of it, was so secure that upon William IV's death, there was no question that the British Empire would be ruled by a queen. And the new queen, Victoria, in her turn, brought the British Empire to heights that were unparalleled in human history.

Chapter Six

Victoria and Saxe-Coburg-Gotha

The reign of Queen Victoria lasted sixty-three years, which was the longest in the history of the British monarchy. During the queen's years on the throne, the British Empire stretched around the globe, including colonies in Africa, India, Australia, New Zealand, Canada, Bermuda, and myriad islands across the seas. By the 1830s it was popular both at home and abroad to refer to it as an empire on which the sun never set.

But when Victoria came to the throne, the monarchy as an institution had developed a reputation for not helping its citizens in need. The second two decades of the nineteenth century had been years of hardship for many Britons, and riots across the country had been met with military force. According to Mike Ashley, although there had been some attempts at reforms to help the underprivileged, "the Hanoverian dynasty . . . had shown little interest

in such progress. There was a general attitude of 'Why bother?' amongst both the royal family and many leading politicians."[48] Additionally, the empire had been subject to the high living and profligate lifestyles of George IV and his brothers. By contrast, Victoria was almost a homebody.

The Princess Alexandrina Victoria

During the scramble to produce heirs in the wake of Princess Charlotte's death in 1817, George III's fourth son, Edward Augustus, the Duke of Kent, had married Mary Louise Victoria, the daughter of Franz I, the German Duke of Saxe-Coburg-Saalfield, in 1818. Edward was fifty, and his new bride was thirty-one. She was recently widowed, with a son and a daughter. Her brother was Prince Leopold, the husband of the late Princess Charlotte. The couple's only child was born in 1819; her parents wanted to christen her Victoire Georgina Alexandrina Charlotte Augusta, but the prince regent insisted that she be called Alexandrina Victoria, in honor of her godfather, Czar Alexander I of Russia. The family, however, always simply called her Victoria.

Her father, who had been prone to fits of cruel temper, died in 1820. Victoria's mother raised her children from both marriages on her own. As a child, Victoria was very close to her half sister Feodora, who was twelve years older, but Feodora left home to be married when Victoria was only nine. The duchess and her adviser, Sir John Conroy, directed Victoria's education under a governess. The princess learned a variety of languages, became a proficient artist and writer, and began keeping a daily journal. Victoria, however, disliked Conroy and felt he had too much influence over her mother. They kept her apart from other children and especially apart from the household of her uncle the king, fearing that William's illegitimate sons and daughters would be a poor influence on Victoria.

Queen Victoria was crowned on June 28, 1837. She would reign for more than sixty-three years.

John Brown

John Brown came into the life of the royal family when Victoria and Albert purchased the Balmoral estate in Scotland in 1847. He served as the prince's assistant during Albert's hunting expeditions. After Albert's death, Brown became Victoria's personal servant.

His outspokenness charmed the mourning queen. He was blunt and honest and helped her emerge from her deep melancholy. She enjoyed his candor and company more than she did that of the nobility and government members who visited her to try to get her to return to public life. He seemed to never leave her side; both friends and family had to go through him to see her. He even foiled an assassination attempt in 1872, tackling a would-be attacker outside the gates of Buckingham Palace.

Their friendship, however, became the subject of intense gossip in London society. There was even a rumor that she had married Brown in a secret ceremony, and wagging tongues referred to her as "Mrs. Brown." The gossip had no effect on Victoria or on Brown. When Brown died in 1883, the queen spoke of his loyal service and abiding friendship, saying that he was "most cruelly missed." Their relationship was the subject of a 1997 movie titled *Mrs. Brown*, starring Judi Dench and Billy Connolly.

Quoted in Howard Cutler. "Victoria's Life in the Highlands." *Masterpiece Theatre*: "Her Majesty Mrs. Brown," n.d. www.pbs.org/wgbh/masterpiece/mbrown/ei_highlands.html.

Ascension to the Throne

Shortly after Victoria's eighteenth birthday, William IV died. In her journal, Victoria recorded how she learned the news on June 20, 1837:

> I was awoke at 6 o'clock by Mamma, who told me that the Archbishop of Canterbury and Lord Conyngham were here, and wished to see me. I got out of bed and went into my sitting-room (only in my dressing-gown), and *alone*, and saw them. Lord Conyngham (the Lord Chamberlain) then acquainted me that my poor Uncle, the King, was no more, and had expired at 12 minutes past 2 this morning, and consequently that I am Queen. . . .
>
> Since it has pleased Providence to place me in this station, I shall do my utmost to fulfil my duty towards my country; I am very young and perhaps in many, though not in all things, inexperienced, but I am sure, that very few have more real good will and more real desire to do what is fit and right than I have.[49]

One of the new queen's first decisions was to get rid of Conroy. Her mother objected strenuously, but Victoria would not be swayed. She had disliked the influence he had had over her mother, and there were even rumors that they had been having an affair. She wanted to make a clean break with the influences of her childhood, and although she allowed her mother to continue to live in the palace, Conroy was exiled from court. It helped show that Victoria was in charge.

Victoria's coronation took place on June 28, 1838, as throngs of Londoners lined the procession route. The queen noted in her journal that because there had not been enough practice before the event, there were a number of errors, particularly among the clergy. She described how a ceremonial ring was placed on the wrong finger and that "the consequence was that I had the greatest difficulty to take it off again,—which I at last did with great pain."[50]

Early Days

Despite the ceremonial gaffes of the coronation, Victoria's reign began smoothly, to the pleasant surprise of many of the leaders of government. The new queen was a refreshing change from her three

Queen Victoria meets with her prime minister, Lord Melbourne. Melbourne gave her solid advice on dealing with Parliament.

immediate Hanoverian predecessors. The kings had been stout, middle-aged, and prone to fits of temper. Victoria was young and thin, with an even temper in conferences. At her first meeting of her Privy Council, the elderly gentlemen were amazed at her composure as she read her opening remarks. Charles Greville, the council's clerk, wrote that the new queen spoke "in a clear, distinct and audible voice, and without any appearance of fear or embarrassment."[51] One of the members, Lord Wellington, observed that her presence "filled the room."[52]

During the first year of her reign, Victoria was guided by two men who became father figures to her. The first was her uncle Leopold, who had become king of Belgium in 1831. He sent her long letters full of advice about the challenges of being a constitutional monarch, including recommendations not to surrender any additional royal prerogatives (powers reserved for exclusive use by the monarch, such as the right to appoint and dismiss a prime minister or to declare war) to Parliament. Leopold's intermittent and abstract advice was supplemented by the day-to-day contact with the prime minister, Lord Melbourne. He provided the young queen with practical everyday recommendations about dealing with the various individuals of the day, as well as supplementing her historical knowledge of the monarchy. She thoroughly enjoyed his company.

Melbourne's advice about dealing with members of Parliament came in good stead when he resigned as prime minister in 1839, following election defeats. Victoria was obliged to invite Sir Robert Peel, leader of the Conservative Party (or Tories), to form a new government, as his party had carried the elections. She had not liked Peel before becoming queen but came to respect him because of Melbourne's influence. During the negotiations over the formation of the new government, Peel insisted on following tradition concerning the queen's ladies in waiting. Peel wanted the current Whig ladies to be replaced by Tories, as a sign of confidence in the new government. Victoria, perhaps remembering Leopold's counsel, refused, saying she never spoke of politics with the women. Peel insisted, but Victoria held firm. As a consequence, Peel declined to become prime minister, and Melbourne returned for the next two years. Although Victoria had won, when Peel's party succeeded in the next elections, she reconsidered her stance. According to historian Jasper Ridley, "Queen Victoria's victory was only temporary, because never again did she challenge the principle that officers of the royal household should change with the government."[53]

While Victoria valued Melbourne's advice about many things related to government, she learned that they did not see eye to eye on what she considered an important issue. She understood that many Britons were poor and believed that the government should help them. Melbourne, like many of his age, believed it was not the government's business. But the young queen soon found someone who shared her interests in social causes, and he became the most important person in her life.

Albert

Victoria first met Prince Albert of the German duchy of Saxe-Coburg-Gotha when his father, her uncle Leopold's brother, brought him to England in 1836.

He was three months younger than the princess, and she was smitten with him from the beginning, although at the time marriage was not on her mind. They shared a number of interests, however, and when he came for a second visit in 1839, after she had become queen, he had matured into a slim and attractive

Victoria and Albert were married in February 1840. The marriage would last until Albert's untimely death at age forty-two. Victoria grieved for him the rest of her life.

The Great Exhibition of 1851

On May 1, 1851, Queen Victoria and Prince Albert arrived in London's Hyde Park to officially open the Great Exhibition of the Works of Industry of All Nations. Albert was president of the commission that had planned the event. They intended it to be an international showcase of the benefits of progress, free trade, and international goodwill. The fair showcased the manufacturing prowess of the British Empire, but also featured art and technological wonders from around the world.

The heart of the Great Exhibition was the Crystal Palace, a soaring four-level iron-and-glass greenhouse that covered 26 acres (10.5ha) of the park. Visitors from all over the world flocked to see it. On one cold and rainy Sunday, an observer from the *Times* of London observed "artisans and shopmen of every class" along with "seamen of different nations who had come from the docks" forming "vast crowds [that] were seen trooping continuously across the park" to attend the fair.

By the time the exhibition closed on October 11, it had been seen by around 6 million people, many of whom returned several times. The queen herself visited it more than thirty times.

Quoted in *Guardian* (Manchester). "The Great Exhibition." May 7, 1851. http://archive.guardian.co.uk/Repository /ml.asp?Ref=R1VBLzE4NTEvMDUvMDcjQXIwMDIwMQ==&Mode=Gif&Locale=english-skin-custom.

Queen Victoria opened the Great Exhibition of 1851 in Hyde Park. The exhibition's highlight was the Crystal Palace (shown), which covered twenty-six acres.

man. She wrote to Leopold, "Albert's beauty is most striking, and he is so amiable and unaffected—in short very *fascinating*."[54]

Victoria asked him to marry her, and he accepted. Their wedding took place in February 1840, and with their marriage, the name Saxe-Coburg-Gotha came into the British royal family. The queen remained part of the House of Hanover, but each of her and Albert's nine children were members of the House of Saxe-Coburg-Gotha. Their first, Princess Victoria, was born in 1840; their second, Edward, the Prince of Wales, was born in 1841. Three boys and four girls followed.

Victoria and Albert were a well-suited team. Because both of their families had been tainted by scandal concerning mistresses, adultery, and illegitimate children, they believed that they should set an example for the kingdom through impeccable behavior. They shared an interest in social issues, such as the conditions of children and workers in the rapidly industrializing nation. Albert's role as prince consort (Parliament refused to grant him the title of king consort), as well as the leadership of prime ministers such as Peel, helped bring about a movement of legislation aimed at social reform. Victoria and Albert were successful at influencing and persuading members of Parliament and other leading politicians. Many of the landmark initiatives that marked Victoria's reign, such as improved standards in education, workplace safety, and public health, were the result of her and Albert's views on ways to improve British society. Additional reforms targeted elections, as the secret ballot was introduced and voting qualifications were expanded, although she opposed movements that advocated granting women the right to vote.

"To Be Cut Off in the Prime of Life"

Victoria and Albert's happy marriage came to a tragic end when he died on December 14, 1861. He was just forty-two. The official cause of death was typhoid fever, although there were no other cases reported in the area. More recent theories point to evidence that Albert had been ill for at least two years before his demise, and that a chronic disease such as cancer or the inflammatory bowel condition called Crohn's disease may have been the real cause of death.

Albert's death devastated Victoria. A week later, she wrote to Leopold, "To be cut off in the prime of life—to see our pure happy, quiet domestic life, which alone enabled me to bear my much disliked position, cut off at forty-two—when I had hoped with such instinctive certainty that God never would part us, and would let us grow old together . . . —is too awful, too cruel!"[55]

Victoria grieved over losing Albert for the rest of her long life, always dressing in the black of mourning. Immediately after his death, she retreated from public life. She refused to make public appearances, and she and her children spent extended periods of time outside London, at family retreats in Scotland

and on the Isle of Wight off the southern coast of England.

By 1864 her isolation was becoming a topic of debate across Britain. When the *Times* reported that she was preparing to return to public life that summer and criticized her for being away so long, she replied in an unsigned letter to the newspaper; the style of the message was unmistakably hers so there was no mystery as to its source. She retorted, "More the Queen could not do, and more the kindness and good feeling of her people would surely not exact of her."[56] Victoria meant that she believed that the demands on her time, particularly regarding public appearances, were overwhelming, and once her people recognized that, they would not begrudge her a continued seclusion.

Victoria and Her Prime Ministers

Although she was out of the public eye, Victoria did not neglect her royal duties. During her withdrawal from public life, she kept abreast of government business and stayed in touch with her prime ministers. Her relationships with them, however, were not always cordial. They tried to convince her that her people needed to see her in public or at state affairs more often. For example, Lord Derby convinced her to address the opening of Parliament in 1866, but she found it a frightening ordeal. Her relationship with the Liberal (formerly Whig) Party's William Gladstone, who was prime minister on four separate occasions from 1868 to 1894, were strained at best; she

found him arrogant and obstinate, calling him a "wild and incomprehensible old fanatic."[57] The Tory Party's Lord Salisbury was more accommodating of the queen's personality, but while the Liberal Lord Rosebery usually acted properly, he was, in the words of British historian Christopher Hibbert, "not always reliable: he required, and was given, frequent lectures [by Victoria] as though he were a schoolboy"[58] for his behavior when dealing with the queen.

By far, the queen's favorite prime minister was the Conservative Party's Benjamin Disraeli. He understood the special nature of dealing with royalty and confided to a friend, "Everyone likes flattery, and when you come to royalty, you should lay it on with a trowel."[59] He spoke to the queen about her writing and poetry, and talked to her about chivalry and gallantry. His ability to engage in subjects other than the tedium of government provided her with valuable diversions, and he helped her emerge from her isolation.

Imperial Britain

The end of Victoria's seclusion was due less to the prodding of her ministers than to the events of a family crisis. In November 1871 Edward, the Prince of Wales, came down with typhoid fever, which was the same illness that the royal doctors and the queen believed had killed Albert. As the tenth anniversary of Albert's death approached, the prince's prognosis was still uncertain. But he eventually improved, and the following February, she and the prince

Queen Victoria poses in the dress she wore for her Golden Jubilee, a celebration of her fiftieth year on the throne. By then Great Britain was the preeminent world power.

attended a public parade through London and a service of thanksgiving for his recovery. The adulation she felt from the cheering crowds perhaps did more to convince her to return to public life than the efforts of her ministers.

By this time, Victoria had been queen for nearly thirty-five years. Over the next fifteen years, her popularity soared. She celebrated fifty years on the throne in 1887 with a series of celebrations called the Golden Jubilee. In that year, the British Empire was the preeminent power on Earth. Victoria's dominions stretched across the globe. British shipping brought raw materials from colonies on six continents to be transported by a complex network of railroads to factories across Britain. Manufactured goods from toys to textiles to tools were then exported to markets around the world. These gains were not, however, without a price. Britain became embroiled in a number of wars during Victoria's reign.

Victorian Wars

Under Victoria, Great Britain was involved in only one European war. In 1854 the Crimean War broke out when Britain and France declared war on Russia in support of the territorial claims of the Ottoman Empire (an empire ruled by Ottoman Turks from the late thirteenth century to 1923 that at its height stretched from southeast Europe through Southwest Asia and the Middle East to northeast Africa). The war eventually led to a treaty in 1856 that greatly favored the Ottoman Empire and its allies, but not before over seventeen thousand British soldiers had died.

Other conflicts involved Britain's far-flung colonies. An uprising in India began in the summer of 1857 when local troops under the British army refused to participate in activities they deemed against their religion. After they were sentenced to long prison terms for insubordination, other native regiments mutinied in what has been called the Indian Mutiny or the Revolt of 1857. Victoria's biographer, Sidney Lee, writing a few years after her death, noted that as the insurrection spread,

The Queen, in common with all her subjects, suffered acute mental torture. She eagerly scanned the news from the disturbed districts, and showered upon her ministers . . . entreaties to do this and that in order to suppress the rebellion with all available speed. . . . "While we are putting off decisions," she wrote to [Prime Minister] Palmerston on September 18, "in the vain *hope* that matters will mend, and in discussing the objections to different measures, the mischief is rapidly progressing, and the time is rapidly progressing, and the time is difficult to catch up again."[60]

The army eventually wore down the resistance. Victoria counseled against indiscriminate punishments and retaliations, and demanded that local customs and religions be respected by the British governors. The uprising led to a reorganization of British rule in India, and was followed by a period of relative calm. Victoria took a great interest in how India was ruled, and in recognition of her efforts, in 1877 Parliament proclaimed her Empress of India.

Violence flared in other colonies as well. In the 1880s Zulus in what is today Sudan rebelled against the British and succeeded in conquering the garrison at Khartoum in January 1885 after a year-long siege. Later rebellions were quelled by British technology and military might. For example, in the Battle of Omdurman in 1898 British troops killed almost ten thousand opposing Sudanese

British technology and military might defeated the Mahdi's army at Omdurman in 1898.

with machine guns and artillery while suffering only forty-seven casualties.

In 1899 a conflict known as the Boer War erupted in the South African colonies in 1899 as groups of descendants of the original Dutch colonists chafed at British rule and sought independence. During this war, as she had done during the Crimean War almost fifty years earlier, Victoria reviewed her troops and visited the wounded in hospitals in Britain. She was undeterred by British losses early in the Boer conflict, proclaiming, "We are not interested in the possibilities of defeat; they do not exist."[61] The British and Boers became locked in a vicious guerrilla war that finally ended with the Boers' defeat in 1902 and the loss of their territory. According to Mike

Ashley, "At that time . . . it would have seemed to Victoria's subjects that Britain ruled the world."[62]

The Close of the Victorian Age

In 1897 Victoria's subjects celebrated sixty years of her rule with her Diamond Jubilee. She had surpassed George III's record for the longest-reigning British monarch. She was now in her late seventies and continued to write in her journal every day. But by 1900 she was suffering from a series of age-related infirmities. Her eyesight was clouded by cataracts and her movements were hindered by rheumatism.

As had been her custom since Albert's death, Victoria spent Christmas of 1900 at Osborne House, her retreat on the Isle of Wight. On January 12, 1901, she wrote in her journal that she had enjoyed an hour's drive around the island. Less than a week later she no longer had the energy to continue her journal after sixty-nine years. She died peacefully on January 22, 1901. She was eighty-one years old.

At the time of her death, Victoria was the only monarch most Britons had ever known. She was considered the grandmother of Europe, and not just because she had reigned for sixty-three years, 216 days. Through her and Albert's children, she was connected to the leading ruling houses of the era. For example, her daughter Victoria was the mother of Kaiser Wilhelm II, the emperor of the German Empire and the king of Prussia. Her second daughter, Alice, was the mother of the wife of Czar Nicholas II, the emperor of Russia. And, upon her death, Victoria and Albert's son Edward, the former Prince of Wales, became head of the House of Saxe-Coburg-Gotha and king of the British Empire.

Edward VII (reigned 1901–1910)

Upon Victoria's death, the Prince of Wales became King Edward VII. He was nearly sixty. His family called him Bertie, as his name was Albert Edward. As he grew up, his parents did not allow him to play any part in royal politics. Although he represented the crown on tours through Europe, Canada, and the United States as a teenager and through India in 1875–1876, the majority of his duties involved the growing royal function of open-

ing buildings, bridges, and other public landmarks. Without any official duties, Edward became a popular figure in society, traveling extensively in Europe to spas, casinos, and horse-racing tracks.

After Albert's death and during Victoria's withdrawal from the public spotlight, Edward had carried on as usual, displaying joviality and delighting in practical jokes. He married Princess Alexandra of Denmark in 1863. She displayed tremendous patience with his affairs with other women, including the famous actress Lily Langtry, which were well-known in society circles but were generally hidden from the public.

Edward played an important part in the planning and preparations of Victoria's Golden Jubilee in 1887 and her Diamond Jubilee in 1897. During his mother's final illness, he was at her side, along with his nephew, Kaiser Wilhelm II. The empire welcomed Edward as king, and his coronation in August was a magnificent affair, with governmental representatives from all over the world in attendance.

Edward the Peacemaker

Like Victoria's reign, Edward's time on the throne was marked by major advances in the welfare of British society, as the government passed legislation that made trade unions legal, implemented a program of national insurance, and established old-age pensions. The king, however, took little personal interest in such matters. He was more interested in foreign affairs, an interest that had been kindled during his extensive visits abroad as the Prince of Wales.

The Funeral of Edward VII

Edward VII's death in 1910 was mourned across the world; the black crepe of mourning adorned windows and lampposts from Paris to Tokyo. Britons wishing to pay their final respects endured drenching rains and lines five miles (8km) long to pass by the late king as he lay in state at Westminster Hall.

The king's funeral on May 20 was one of the largest gatherings of European royalty ever to occur. The gun carriage bearing his casket was followed by his horse and by his wirehaired terrier. Three men followed on horseback: the new king, his son George V; the king's brother, the Duke of Connaught; and the late king's nephew, Kaiser Wilhelm II. The king's widow, her children, and the new king's wife and family followed in carriages. Other carriages carried five heirs apparent, seven current or widowed queens, forty imperial or royal highnesses, and representatives from nations around the world, including U.S. president Theodore Roosevelt.

It seemed to mark the end of an era. The historian Lord Esher wrote in his diary afterward, "There was never such a breakup. All the old buoys which have marked the channel of our lives seem to have been swept away."

Quoted in Barbara Tuchman. *The Guns of August*. Anniversary ed. New York: Macmillan, 1988, p. 14.

One of the hallmarks of Edward's reign was his effort to promote goodwill among the nations of Europe. He succeeded in continuing the positive relations with France that Victoria had begun, leading to the *Entente cordiale* (friendly agreement) between the two nations in 1904. He made state visits to Paris, France; Athens, Greece; Oslo, Norway; and Stockholm, Sweden, and met with his nephew Czar Nicholas II at the Baltic seaport of Tallinn in 1908.

His efforts to keep the peace through these goodwill efforts led to the nickname Edward the Peacemaker in Britain. His efforts were less well received in Germany, where his nephew, the kaiser, saw Edward's efforts as attempts to create agreements that eventually would threaten German interests in trade, colonial expansion, and international relations. This growing anti-British animosity in Germany would come to a head in the coming decade.

Edward, however, did not live to see these events come to pass. He died on May 6, 1910, from bronchial complications likely related to his smoking habit. He was sixty-eight. His eldest son, Albert, had died from pneumonia in 1892 in his late twenties; his second son, George, ascended to the throne as George V.

Chapter Seven

The House of Windsor

With the dawning of the twentieth century, the British monarchy was firmly in the hands of the House of Saxe-Coburg-Gotha. Edward VII had lived long enough to see several grandsons born, so the line of succession was secure. His younger son, George, was, by the time of Edward's death, the heir apparent. Earlier in his life, between 1877 and 1892, George had served in the British navy and traveled all over the world, serving on vessels that sailed to the Caribbean, South America, Australia, Japan, and China. He had been on furlough in 1892 when the news of his older brother's death reached him. He had to put aside his life as a sailor to prepare to someday succeed his father.

In July 1893 George married Princess Victoria Mary of Teck, known to the family simply as Mary. Although she was the daughter of a German prince, she had been born and raised in England. George and Mary's first son, Edward Albert, known to the family as David, was born in 1894, and a second son, Albert, arrived in 1895. Three more sons and a daughter followed between 1897 and 1905. George and Mary were well suited to each other and a devoted couple whose marriage lasted forty-three years.

George and his father had good relations, unlike previous generations of father and heir apparent. Edward ensured that his son was prepared for the throne; he shared with George the important state documents and counseled him on courses of action. When Edward died in 1910, the heir apparent became George V.

George V (reigned 1910–1936)

The greatest test of George V's leadership skills came in 1914 with the outbreak of what is now called World War I, and he rose to the challenge. George and Great Britain were allied with his cousin Czar Nicholas II of Russia, but against his cousin Kaiser Wilhelm II of Germany. He and Queen Mary shared the same food rationing as their subjects. During the four years of the war, he made more than four hundred trips to both army and navy installations, more than three hundred visits to field hospitals, and numerous tours of factories, helping to further the war effort and to boost morale. He said to the troops

King George V (right) is pictured with his cousin Russian czar Nicholas II at the wedding of the German kaiser's daughter in 1913. A year later Great Britain and Russia would be at war with Germany.

The House of Windsor

During World War I, King George V's House of Saxe-Coburg-Gotha had an image problem. The savagery of the war had led to an intense hatred of all things German. Stores with German-sounding names were looted, and individuals with Germanic last names were suspected of espionage. For the royal family, these actions came close to home when Prince Louis of Battenburg, a cousin of the king, was harassed into resigning his post of First Sea Lord (secretary of the navy).

On July 17, 1917, King George decided to address the problem with a royal proclamation that declared,

> Now, therefore, We, out of Our Royal Will and Authority, do hereby declare and announce that as from the date. . . . Our House and Family shall be styled and known as the House and Family of Windsor, and that all the descendants in the male line of Our said Grandmother Queen Victoria who are subjects of these Realms, other than female descendants who may marry or may have married, shall bear the said Name of Windsor.

The new name came from the iconic Windsor Castle and remains the name of the royal family to this day.

Quoted in *London Gazette*, July 17, 1917, p. 1. www.london-gazette.co.uk/issues/30186/pages/7119.

on the front lines, "I cannot share your hardships, but my heart is with you every hour of the day."[63]

Although Britain and its allies were victorious, the war was not without personal heartache for the king. During the upheavals of the Russian Revolution in 1917, Nicholas II and his wife (George's cousin Alice, known in Russia as Alexandra Feodorovna) and all their children were murdered by socialist revolutionaries. George was devastated. His cousin the kaiser was luckier; he fled Germany after its defeat and lived out the rest of his days in the Netherlands. As Mike Ashley observes, "The old Europe was crumbling and Victoria's descendants were being replaced."[64] In Britain, however, the monarchy not only weathered the storm, but by the end of George's reign, it was as popular as ever.

New Forces, New Challenges

The postwar years presented new challenges to George and Great Britain. One was the centuries-old question of Irish independence. Ireland had been under varying degrees of English and then British control for centuries. Some monarchs had tried to subjugate the Irish through military means, while others had encouraged English settlement, hoping to create a pro-English colony. Under Victoria, members of Parliament unsuccessfully tried to enact measures to grant Ireland a measure of independence. In 1916 anti-British militants led an uprising, which was crushed by the British army, resulting in further calls for freedom from royal rule. In the 1918 Parliamentary elections, the Sinn Fein Party, which advocated independence from Great Britain, won sweeping victories throughout the island. The new members refused to attend Parliament, and instead created their own legislature in the city of Dublin. For the next three years, the Irish Republican Army (which was in favor of independence) and the Royal Irish Constabulary (of the British government) fought guerrilla campaigns of assassinations, bombings, and street fighting. In hopes of bringing peace to Ireland, George encouraged prime minister David Lloyd George to be generous in resolving the question of independence. In the words of historian Andrew Roberts, King George "wanted every possible effort to ensure that the new self-governing [Republic of Ireland] should be born with as little bitterness as possible."[65] Negotiations led to a truce, and in 1921 the majority of Ireland became independent, although six counties in the north chose to stay with Britain as the province of Northern Ireland.

The kingdom's political landscape changed as well with the rise of the pro-working-class Labour Party, which first led the nation under prime minister Ramsey MacDonald in 1924. The king's very conservative nature did not keep him from working with the liberal MacDonald, and he grew to admire and respect the Scotsman. In 1931 George promoted the idea of a "national government," a coalition of the Labour, Conservative, and Liberal parties, to help the nation through the Great Depression.

On December 25, 1932, George took on another new challenge when he took to the radio to make the first of his Christmas greeting broadcasts to the nation and the empire. It was the beginning of a tradition that remains to this day. These messages, as well as newsreels of George and Mary shown in theaters, helped connect the monarchy to the people as never before. Consequently, at his Silver Jubilee celebrations in 1935, marking twenty-five years on the throne, George was showered with thanks and affection.

The king's health, however, was declining. He made a final Christmas address on December 25, 1935, before developing a severe bronchial infection in January. He died on January 20, 1936. He had seen his country through one world war, social upheaval, and economic turbulence, and today is considered one of Britain's most important kings. He was succeeded by his son David, the Prince of Wales.

Edward VIII (reigned 1936)

Edward VIII, known as David to his family, was born on June 23, 1894, the eldest son of the future George V. His great-grandmother, Queen Victoria, doted on him. It was the first time in British history that four generations of the monarchy were alive at the same time.

David became the House of Windsor's Prince of Wales in 1911, and served in the army behind the lines during World War I. After the war, in 1919 and 1920, he was sent on tours of the United States and the dominions of Canada, Australia, New Zealand, and India to help promote goodwill and international relations. The international press found him dashing and outspoken and reported his every move. He moved in a circle of society that favored thrills and fast living. His good looks were offset by an apparent penchant for brooding during official functions; in most cases, he was just bored.

On a tour of the United States in 1931, he met a married divorcée named Wallis Simpson. By 1935 they were in love. On Easter Day 1935 he wrote to her, "I love you more & more & more each & every minute & miss you so terribly here. You do too don't you my sweetheart?"[66] The prince, however, never found the right time to tell his father the news.

Abdicating for "the Woman I Love"

When George V died, few in Britain outside the government and David's friends knew about Mrs. Simpson. The British press had agreed not to mention her until the prince became king, but the American and European press had written about her all along. By summer 1936 his affair was common knowledge even in Britain. The new king, who called himself Edward VIII, believed that the British would accept an American as queen, even though she was now twice divorced and both husbands were still living. Edward's mother, the former Queen Mary, along with the Archbishop of Canterbury and members of the government, disagreed and tried to get him to end the relationship.

In October 1936 the prime minister, Stanley Baldwin, gave Edward a collection of press clippings from around the world, documenting the affair. Baldwin pointed out that a king under a constitutional monarchy was more dependent on integrity and goodwill than ever before. On November 16, the king informed Baldwin that he had made a decision. He was prepared to abdicate, preferring to give up the throne of the British Empire rather than to lose Mrs. Simpson.

On December 10 Edward abdicated. That evening, in a radio broadcast, he told the nation that "I have found it impossible to carry the heavy burden of responsibility and to discharge my duties as king as I would wish to do without the help and support of the woman I love."[67] His younger brother Albert, the Duke of York, ascended the throne. He chose the name George VI in honor of his father.

George VI (reigned 1936–1952)

The new king, the former Prince Albert, had had a difficult childhood. As the second son of George and Mary, he had received less attention than his older brother David, who had an abundance

Former king Edward VIII poses with his commoner wife, Wallis Simpson, after their wedding in 1937. On December 10, 1936, in a radio address to the nation Edward abdicated the throne in order to marry Simpson.

of charm and good looks. The young Albert suffered from gastritis and was forced to walk with leg braces to try to correct his knock-kneed condition. Perhaps it is not surprising that by the age of eight he had developed a stutter that became extremely pronounced under stress.

In 1922 he met Lady Elizabeth Bowles-Lyon. She was not a member of a British or European royal family, but her family traced its roots back to a Welsh prince on

The Duke and Duchess of Windsor

After his abdication, the former King Edward VIII was granted the title of the Duke of Windsor. He and Wallis Simpson were married in 1937; she thus became the Duchess of Windsor. They lived in Paris until 1940 and escaped to Portugal when France was occupied during World War II. The duke was appointed the governor of the Bahamas, a post he held until 1945.

The couple then returned to Paris, where they lived for the rest of their lives in-between travels abroad. Many of the royal family had no wish to see them. King George VI's wife, Queen Elizabeth, was particularly harsh, blaming her husband's premature death on their affair. Under Queen Elizabeth II, however, relations improved, and the duke and duchess attended several state functions in England in the 1960s.

The duke suffered from ill health and by the time the queen visited him and his wife during a state visit to France in April 1972, he was dying of cancer. He died on May 28, 1972, and was buried at Windsor Castle. The duchess died in 1986 after suffering from senile dementia for many years and was buried by his side.

one side and a Scots lord on the other. They were married the following year. They had a happy marriage and had two daughters: Elizabeth, born in 1926, and Margaret, born in 1930.

With his wife's support, and professional speech therapy, George began to manage his stutter. Although he never fully overcame it, he learned techniques to deal with the stress of formal speeches and radio addresses with only minimal difficulty. But he was not prepared for his brother's abdication, nor was he ready to be king.

"In This Grave Hour"

As the new king, George immediately set about learning all he needed to know about the state of the government and, in particular, the state of international affairs. He dearly hoped a political solution could be found to avoid another European war, but when World War II began, George VI took to the airwaves on September 3, 1939, to address his people about the challenges ahead. He counseled that "in this grave hour, perhaps the most fateful in our history," the British people needed "to stand calm, firm, and united in this time of trial."[68]

George and Elizabeth were inspired by the examples of George V and Queen Mary for helping the nation in a time of war. They chose to stay in London despite German air raids, even in the wake of six bombs that hit Buckingham

Palace in September 1940. One detonated thirty yards (27m) from where the king was attending a meeting. The king and queen visited the worst-hit areas of the city, and their concern brought them widespread public acclaim. The king visited the armed forces throughout the war, including trips to North Africa, Italy, and France.

The war in Europe came to a close with Germany's surrender on May 8, 1945. That same day, the king made a radio address, in which he thanked his people for their efforts but reminded them, "Much hard work awaits us, both in the restoration of our own country after the ravages of war and in helping to restore peace and sanity to a shattered world."[69]

Endings and Beginnings

The postwar world brought a number of significant changes to the British Empire and the monarchy. The changes had begun in 1931 with the formation of the Commonwealth of Nations, an association of Great Britain, Canada, Australia, New Zealand, and South Africa, former colonies that were now independent. The nations of the Commonwealth recognized the king as "the symbol of the free association of the Independent Member Nations and as such Head of the Commonwealth"[70]

King George VI stands with his wife, Elizabeth, and daughters, Princess Elizabeth and Princess Margaret, on the balcony of Buckingham Palace shortly after his coronation.

while maintaining responsibility over their own governments.

After the war other territories of the empire desired independence as well. For example, in 1947 Britain agreed to end British rule in India. The territory became two new nations, India and Pakistan. George VI surrendered his title of Emperor of India, and both India and Pakistan joined the Commonwealth to retain ties to the monarchy.

The postwar years also brought changes to the king's family. In 1947 Princess Elizabeth married Philip Mountbatten. Philip was the son of Prince Andrew of Greece, who had been exiled by a military coup in 1922 and had been raised by his English uncle, Lord Mountbatten. After the wedding, George wrote to his daughter that "our family, us four, the 'Royal Family' must remain together, with additions of course at suitable moments! . . . Your leaving us has left a great blank in our lives but do remember that your old home is still yours."[71] The family's first "suitable addition" came with the birth of Elizabeth and Philip's son Charles in 1948, followed by a daughter, Anne, in 1950.

The king's health declined in the following years. He saw Elizabeth and Philip off on an overseas goodwill tour in late January 1952, but a week later, on February 6, 1952, the couple learned that the king had died in his sleep the night before. King George VI was only fifty-six when he died. Thrust unexpectedly and unwillingly into the role of king, he had worked wonders to restore the image of the monarchy after his brother's abdi-cation and had shown true leadership throughout the war. Now that mantle of leadership was placed upon the shoulders of his twenty-five-year-old daughter, Elizabeth.

Elizabeth II (reigns 1952–)

Princess Elizabeth Alexandra Mary was born on April 21, 1926. As a teenager, she had stayed in London with her parents during the German attacks of World War II. In 1945, at the age of eighteen, she enlisted in the Auxiliary Territorial Service, the women's branch of the British army at the time, where she learned how to handle and repair a wide variety of vehicles. Her wedding to Philip Mountbatten was broadcast live over the radio and, upon her insistence, on television as well. She and Philip were abroad in Kenya in 1952 when the news reached them of the king's death. The newsreel and television cameras caught her as she emerged from the airplane the next day, dressed in mourning black and greeting members of the government. On February 8, she was proclaimed Queen Elizabeth II.

The new queen's coronation was televised live on June 2, 1953, and was seen by 20 million viewers across Britain. Elizabeth and Philip's second son, Andrew, was born in 1960, and a third, Edward, followed in 1964. The couple's children were the first members of the royal family to be educated outside the home, attending regular schools and universities. It was another example of the continuing evolution of the British monarchy.

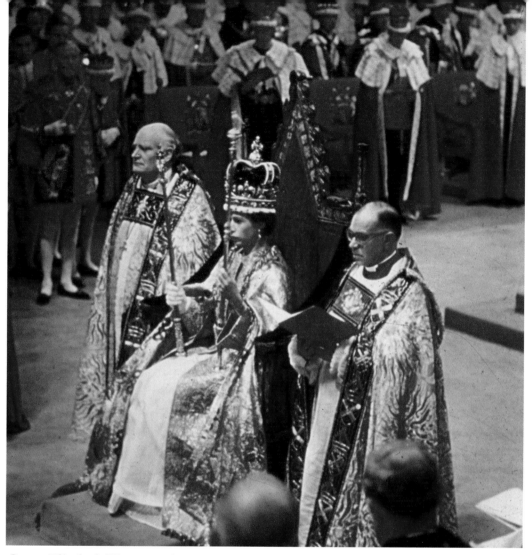

Queen Elizabeth II's coronation ceremony on June 2, 1953, was watched by 20 million British and millions of others worldwide.

Leadership in a Constitutional Monarchy

During the first decades of Elizabeth's rule, she worked to foster better relations among the nations of the Commonwealth. Throughout the 1950s and 1960s, many former territories of the British Empire gained their independence, particularly in Africa. By 1970 the Commonwealth had grown to thirty-two nations and by 2011, there were fifty-four nations that recognized Elizabeth either as the head of state or as the head of the Commonwealth, a ceremonial position (i.e., without governing power) that is hers for life.

Throughout her reign, Elizabeth has continued to make countless overseas tours to foster goodwill among the Commonwealth nations. In 1953 she began a six-month tour around the world, becoming the first reigning monarch to visit Australia and New Zealand. She has visited Canada more than a dozen times and made a thirteenth visit to Australia in late 2011.

Today, in her late eighties, the queen spends the bulk of her time in Britain. She meets with the prime minister regularly, usually once a week, to receive updates on government affairs and to share views on current issues. Many have discovered the queen's skill at keeping up with the times. Tony Blair, her prime minister from 1997 to 2007, commented, "What I found to be her most surprising attribute is how streetwise she is. Frequently, throughout my time as prime minister, I was stunned by her total ability to pick up the public mood."[72] Former prime minister Sir John Major (1990–1997) agrees, saying, "There's very little she hasn't seen. In my own experience, there's almost nothing that ruffles her."[73]

Family Leadership

The queen is also the leader of the House of Windsor. Elizabeth has needed to juggle the roles and obligations of the monarchy with those of her family. As queen and as head of the Church of England, she had to advise her sister, Princess Margaret, in 1953 that Margaret's planned marriage to a divorced man was against church practices at the time. Margaret eventually married in 1960, but that marriage ended in divorce.

Margaret's divorce came amid accusations of extramarital affairs, which also plagued the marriage of Charles, the Prince of Wales, to Lady Diana Spencer. The prince, thirty-two, and Diana, nineteen, were married in a highly publicized ceremony on July 29, 1981. The event was broadcast worldwide and was watched by 750 million viewers. Their first son, Prince William, was born in 1982 and their second, Prince Henry (known as Harry), was born in 1984. But the seemingly idyllic marriage began to fray as Charles continued a relationship with an old flame, Camilla Parker Bowles. In response, Diana had affairs as well. Charles and Diana formally separated in 1992.

"Annus Horribilis"

The year 1992 was particularly trying for the queen. Her daughter, Princess Anne, divorced her husband, Mark Philips, after nearly twenty years of marriage, amid allegations that Anne was having an affair with a member of the royal staff (which she was, and whom she subsequently married). Her second son, Prince Andrew, separated from his wife, Sarah Ferguson, after less than six years of marriage. In addition, in the fall of 1992, there was a devastating fire at the royal residence at Windsor Castle. Elizabeth summed up the events of the year in a speech at the Guildhall, the ceremonial center of the Corporation of the City of London. She said, "In the words of one of my more sympathetic correspondents, it has turned out to be an annus horribilis,"[74] Latin for "a horrible year."

There were, however, more public troubles to come. Charles and Diana were unable to reconcile, and after con-

"The Queen Mum"

One of the iconic figures of the British monarchy in the last century was Queen Elizabeth, the Queen Mother. She was the widow of King George VI and mother of Queen Elizabeth II. After her daughter's ascension, Elizabeth represented the crown during special ceremonies, such as dedicating monuments or opening events, which she continued throughout her long life.

The Queen Mother turned one hundred years of age in August 2000. She received accolades and congratulations from across the kingdom and around the world. Her final public appearance came in November 2001, when she spent three hours touring the aircraft carrier HMS *Ark Royal*. She developed a cold later that month that lingered and died peacefully on March 30, 2002, having reached the age of 101. Her daughter the queen was at her side.

Her legacy, however, goes far beyond her status as queen consort and mother of the queen. To many Britons, she was their beloved "Queen Mum." Her popularity was based on her good humor, her witty turns of phrase, and her seemingly unflappable nature. For many, she was a symbol of Britain's decency and courage. When she died, prime minister Tony Blair said, "She was admired by all people of all ages and backgrounds, revered within our borders and beyond."

Quoted on BBC News, March 30, 2002. www.youtube.com/watch?v=UC0SqYYQmIM.

The "Queen Mum" was much beloved by Britons as a symbol of decency and courage.

sulting the prime minister and the archbishop of Canterbury about the feasibility of a divorce, Elizabeth ordered Charles to dissolve the marriage. Charles and Diana were formally divorced in 1996; he married Camilla in 2005.

Diana was killed in an automobile crash in Paris in 1997. The tragic death brought the queen into the spotlight again. Elizabeth and her family chose to mourn privately at her estate in Scotland, Balmoral, where they were when

"Simply by Order of Birth"

On October 28, 2011, prime minister David Cameron announced a new landmark practice that would affect the future of the British monarchy. Speaking at a conference of Commonwealth nations in Australia, Cameron announced that the sixteen Commonwealth nations that recognize Queen Elizabeth II as their head of state had agreed to change the policies surrounding heirs to the throne: "I'm very pleased to say that we've reached a unanimous agreement on changes to the rules of succession. We will end the male primogeniture rule so that in future the order of succession should be determined simply by order of birth."[1]

The change is likely due in part to the wedding of Prince William and Catherine "Kate" Middleton in April 2011, as William is second in line to inherit the throne. The measure must be approved by the parliaments of all sixteen nations. In Great Britain approval will require the amendment of a series of laws already in effect, dating back to at least 1689. One British account of the change noted that "the legal changes are not expected to come in for at least another four years—and by then we may well know if, for [William and Catherine], they have made any difference at all."[2]

1. Quoted in Newsy. "British Monarchy Ends Discrimination of Elder Sisters." October 29, 2011. www .newsy.com/videos/british-monarchy-ends-discrimination-of-elder-sisters.
2. BBC News UK. "Overturning Centuries of Royal Rules." October 28, 2011. www.bbc.co.uk/news /uk-15489544.

they heard the news. Many in the public felt the queen should have made a public announcement immediately. The day before Diana's funeral, the queen released a televised statement in tribute to the late princess, and she bowed her head as Diana's casket passed her at the ceremony. It provided a measure of comfort to those who mourned Diana and who felt the queen did not share their grief.

In February 2002 Princess Margaret, the queen's younger sister, died after a series of strokes at the age of 71. Less than six weeks later, Elizabeth's mother, affectionately known as "the Queen Mum," died at 101. Consequently, her daughter's Golden Jubilee celebrations, which culminated with celebrations in August, were tinged with a bit of melancholy. Elizabeth and Philip, however, continued with the scheduled events, which included a range of trips overseas and parties at royal estates. According to the monarchy's website, "Around 160,000 cups of tea, 54,000 drop scones and 48,000 slices of chocolate and lemon cake were served at Jubilee Garden Parties"[75] that summer.

The Enduring Monarchy

The presence of a royal website reflects the continuing evolution of the British monarchy. The monarchy also has an official Facebook page and a channel on YouTube. A news story in September 2011 featured Prince Charles having a video chat via Skype at a technology center. That same month prime minister David Cameron, finding the queen playing solitaire, tried to impress her by showing her she could do the same on an iPad. The queen told him that although she had heard about the iPad, she preferred to use regular playing cards. Her opinion demonstrates the mixture of the traditional and the modern that has marked Elizabeth's reign for sixty years.

The queen turned eighty-six in April 2012, and she continues to maintain a full schedule. In fact, between 2005 and 2010 the number of events hosted by Elizabeth and her family at Buckingham Palace grew by 50 percent. Her personal appearances in 2010 were up 20 percent from the year before. Her grandson, Prince William, the Duke of Cambridge, marvels at her energy and spirit. With a grin, he remarks that he and his father, the Prince of Wales, and the queen's other children have raised the subject of the queen's hectic schedule, saying, "It's a bit difficult for us to say 'take it easy' when she's so much older than us and has done so much more. We do hint at taking some [duties] off her, but she won't have anything of it."[76]

For Queen Elizabeth II, duty and country are everything. Since the deaths of Princess Margaret and the Queen Mother in 2002, however, she has become more than just the queen. She is, in Sir John Major's words, "the mother of the nation."[77] Perhaps Prince William sums up the queen's legacy best:

> It's about setting examples. It's about doing one's duty, as she would say. It's about using your position for the good. It's about serving the country—and that really is the crux of it all. . . . For her, it must be a relief to know that she has furrowed her own path and that she's done it successfully, and that the decisions she's made have turned out to be correct. You make it up a lot as you go along. So to be proven right when it's your decision-making gives you a lot of confidence. You realize that the role you're doing—you're doing it well; that you're making a difference. That's what's key. It's about making a difference for the country.[78]

Notes

Introduction: A Royal Wedding

1. Quoted in *Time*. "The Relationship." The Royal Wedding, May 16, 2011, p. 44.
2. Quoted in *Time*. "Kate and William." The Royal Wedding, May 16, 2011, p. 35.

Chapter One: Medieval England

3. Quoted in John Gillingham. "The Normans: William II, 1087–1100." In *The Lives of the Kings & Queens of England*, edited by Antonia Fraser. Berkeley and Los Angeles: University of California Press, 1999, p. 27.
4. Mike Ashley. *A Brief History of British Kings & Queens*. Philadelphia: Running Press, 2008, p. 67.
5. Quoted in Gillingham, "The Normans: Stephen, 1135–54," p. 39.
6. Quoted in Ashley. *A Brief History*, p. 127.
7. Gillingham. "The Angevins: Richard I, 1189–1199," p. 60.
8. Ashley. *A Brief History*, pp. 136–137.
9. Ralph V. Turner and Richard H. Heiser. *The Reign of Richard Lionheart: Ruler of the Angevin Empire, 1189–1199*. Harlow, UK: Pearson Education, 2000, p. 248.
10. Peter Earle. "The Plantagenets: Henry III, 1216–1272." In *The Lives of the Kings & Queens of England*, p. 78.

Chapter Two: The Plantagenets and the Wars of the Roses

11. Ashley. *A Brief History*, p. 170.
12. Earle. "The Plantagenets: Edward I, 1272–1307," p. 86.
13. Quoted in Brian L. Blakeley and Jacquelin Collins. *Documents in British History*. Vol. I: *Early Times to 1714*. 2nd ed. New York: McGraw-Hill, 1993, p. 91.
14. Miri Rubin. *The Hollow Crown: A History of Britain in the Late Middle Ages*. New York: Penguin, 2005, p. 173.
15. Quoted in Anthony Cheetham. "The House of Lancaster: Henry IV, 1399–1213." In *The Lives of the Kings & Queens of England*, p. 119.
16. Ashley. *A Brief History*, p. 205.
17. Rubin. *The Hollow Crown*, p. 272.
18. Quoted in Cheetham. "The House of Lancaster: Henry VI, 1422–1471," p. 135.
19. Cheetham. "The House of York: Richard III 1483–1485," p. 158.

Chapter Three: The House of Tudor

20. Ashley. *A Brief History*, p. 233.

21. Quoted in Leslie Carroll. *Royal Affairs: A Lusty Romp Through the Extramarital Affairs That Rocked the British Monarchy*. New York: New American Library, 2008, p. 81.
22. John Cannon and Ralph Griffiths. *The Oxford Illustrated History of the British Monarchy*. New York: Oxford University Press, 1988, p. 325.
23. Quoted in Emily Sohn. "King Henry VIII's Madness Explained," *Discovery News*, March 11, 2011. http://news.discovery.com/history/henry-viii-blood-disorder-110311.html.
24. Cannon and Griffiths. *The Oxford Illustrated History of the British Monarchy*, p. 330.
25. Quoted in Neville Williams. "The Tudors: Elizabeth I, 1558–1603." In *The Lives of the Kings & Queens of England*, p. 203.
26. Quoted in Luminarium: Anthology of English Literature. "Queen Elizabeth I of England: Speech to the Troops at Tilbury." www.luminarium.org/renlit/tilbury.htm.

Chapter Four: The Struggle for Power

27. Quoted in Cannon and Griffiths. *The Oxford Illustrated History of the British Monarchy*, p. 386.
28. Ashley. *A Brief History*, p. 314.
29. Henry Sidney et al. "Invitation to William," June 30, 1688. http://history.wisc.edu/sommerville/351/WIIIinvite.html.
30. Maurice Ashley. "The Stuarts: James II, 1685–8." In *The Lives of the Kings & Queens of England*, p. 246.
31. Quoted in The Official Website of the British Monarchy. *History of the Monarchy:United Kingdom Monarchs (1603–Present); The Stuarts*. "William III (r. 1689–1702) and Mary II (r. 1689–1694)." www.royal.gov.uk/HistoryoftheMonarchy/KingsandQueensoftheUnitedKingdom/TheStuarts/MaryIIWilliamIIIandTheActofSettlement/MaryIIWilliamIII.aspx.
32. Quoted in Ashley. "The Stuarts: William III 1688–1702 and Mary 1688–94," p. 253.
33. Quoted in Cannon and Griffiths. *The Oxford Illustrated History of the British Monarchy*, p. 439.
34. Ashley. *A Brief History*, p. 336.
35. Quoted in Cannon and Griffiths. *The Oxford Illustrated History of the British Monarchy*, p. 459.

Chapter Five: The Hanoverian Succession

36. Cannon and Griffiths. *The Oxford Illustrated History of the British Monarchy*, p. 459.
37. Ashley. *A Brief History*, p. 349.
38. Ashley. *A Brief History*, p. 353.
39. Quoted in Cannon and Griffiths. *The Oxford Illustrated History of the British Monarch*, p. 480.
40. Quoted in John Clarke. "The House of Hanover: George II, 1727–60." In *The Lives of the Kings & Queens of England*, p. 278.
41. Quoted in Clarke. "The House of Hanover: George III, 1760–1820," p. 284.
42. Quoted in Cannon and Griffiths. *The Oxford Illustrated History of the British Monarch*, p. 511.

43. Ashley. *A Brief History*, p. 362.

44. Quoted in Brycchan Carey's Website. "Sancho Describes the Gordon Riots, June 6, 1780." www.brycch ancarey.com/sancho/letter2.htm.

45. Quoted in Cannon and Griffiths. *The Oxford Illustrated History of the British Monarchy*, p. 529.

46. Quoted in Clarke. "The House of Hanover: William IV, 1830–7," p. 296.

47. Quoted in The Official Website of the British Monarchy. "William IV (r. 1830–1837)." *History of the Monarchy: United Kingdom Monarchs (1603–Present); The Hanoverians.* www.royal.gov.uk/Historyofthe Monarchy/KingsandQueensofthe UnitedKingdom/TheHanoverians /WilliamIV.aspx.

Chapter Six: Victoria and Saxe-Coburg-Gotha

48. Ashley. *A Brief History*, p. 372.

49. Quoted in The Official Website of the British Monarchy. Queen Victoria. *Historic Royal Speeches and Writings: Queen Victoria (r. 1837–1901).* "On William IV's Death, and Her Accession Aged 18 Years: Tuesday, 20 June 1837 at Kensington Palace." www.royal.gov.uk/pdf/victoria .pdf.

50. Quoted in The Official Website of the British Monarchy. Queen Victoria. *Historic Royal Speeches and Writings: Queen Victoria (r. 1837–1901).* "Coronation: June 28, 1838." www .royal.gov.uk/pdf/victoria.pdf.

51. Quoted in Cannon and Griffiths. *The Oxford Illustrated History of the British Monarchy*, p. 551.

52. Quoted in Cannon and Griffiths. *The Oxford Illustrated History of the British Monarchy,* p. 551.

53. Jasper Ridley. "The House of Hanover: Victoria, 1837–1901." In *The Lives of the Kings & Queens of England*, p. 301.

54. Quoted in Cannon and Griffiths. *The Oxford Illustrated History of the British Monarchy*, p. 555.

55. Quoted in The Official Website of the British Monarchy. Queen Victoria. *Historic Royal Speeches and Writings: Queen Victoria (r. 1837–1901).* "The Death of Queen Victoria's Beloved Husband, Prince Albert. . . ." www.royal.gov.uk/pdf/victoria .pdf.

56. Quoted in Cannon and Griffiths. *The Oxford Illustrated History of the British Monarchy*, p. 563.

57. Quoted in Christopher Hibbert. "Queen Victoria and Her Prime Ministers." *BBC History*, February 17, 2011. www.bbc.co.uk/history /british/victorians/victoria_min isters_01.shtml.

58. Hibbert. "Queen Victoria and Her Prime Ministers."

59. Quoted in Ridley. "The House of Hanover: Victoria, 1837–1901," p. 313.

60. Sidney Lee. *Queen Victoria: A Biography.* London: Smith, Elder, 1903, pp. 275–276.

61. Quoted in The Official Website of the British Monarchy. "Victoria (r. 1837–1901)." *History of the Monarchy: United Kingdom Monarchs (1603–Present); The Hanoverians.* www.royal.gov.uk/Historyofthe Monarchy/KingsandQueensoft

heUnitedKingdom / TheHanoveri
ans / Victoria.aspx.

62. Ashley. *A Brief History*, p. 380.

Chapter Seven: The House of Windsor

63. Quoted in Andrew Roberts. "The House of Windsor: George V, 1910–36." In *The Lives of the Kings & Queens of England*, p. 336.

64. Ashley. *A Brief History*, p. 393.

65. Roberts. "The House of Windsor: George V," p. 338.

66. Quoted in Cannon and Griffiths. *The Oxford Illustrated History of the British Monarchy*, p. 604.

67. The Official Website of the British Monarchy. Edward, Duke of Windsor. "Broadcast After His Abdication, 11 December 1936." *Historic Royal Speeches and Writings: Edward VIII (r. Jan–December 1936).* www .royal.gov.uk / pdf / edwardviii.pdf.

68. George VI, September 3, 1939. *Historic Royal speeches and writings: George VI (r. 1936-1952),* "Broadcast, outbreak of war with Germany, 3 September 1939." www.royal.gov .uk / pdf / georgevi.pdf.

69. The Official Website of the British Monarchy. George VI. "Broadcast, VE (Victory in Europe) Day, 8 May 1945." *Historic Royal Speeches and Writings: George VI (r. 1936–1952).* www.royal.gov.uk / pdf / georgevi .pdf.

70. The Official Website of the British Monarchy. "Origins of the Commonwealth." 2009. *The Queen and the Commonwealth: About the Commonwealth.* www.royal.gov.uk / MonarchAndCommonwealth / TheCommonwealth / Originsofthe Commonwealth.aspx.

71. Quoted in Cannon and Griffiths. *The Oxford Illustrated History of the British Monarchy*, p. 614.

72. Quoted in Robert Hardman. "From the Unwelcome Visitor at the Palace to the Joy of Losing Herself in a Crowd . . . Robert Hardman Reveals the Private Side of a Thoroughly Modern Monarch." *Daily Mail,* September 25, 2011. www.daily mail.co.uk / news / article-2041776 / Queen-Elizabeth-Private-thor oughly-modern-monarch.html.

73. Quoted in Hardman. "From the Unwelcome Visitor at the Palace. . . ."

74. Quoted in Roberts. "The House of Windsor: Elizabeth II, 1952–," p. 368.

75. The Official Website of the British Monarchy. "50 Facts about the Queen's Golden Jubilee," www .royal.gov.uk / HMTheQueen / The Queenandspecialanniversaries / TheQueensGoldenJubilee / 50fac tsaboutTheQueensGoldenJubilee .aspx.

76. Quoted in Robert Hardman. "'My Grandma Is Incredible,' Says Prince William in Exclusive, Unprecedented and Candid Interview with Author and Journalist Robert Hardman." *Daily Mail,* September 23, 2011. www.dailymail.co.uk / news / article-2041213 / Prince-William -Queen-Elizabeth-exclusive-inter view--My-grandma-incredible .html?ito=feeds-newsxml.

77. Quoted in Hardman. "From the Unwelcome Visitor at the Palace. . . ."

78. Quoted in Hardman. "'My Grandma Is Incredible. . . .'"

For More Information

Books

Mike Ashley. *A Brief History of British Kings and Queens*. Philadelphia: Running Press, 2008. Brief but insightful biographical sketches of the kings and queens of England, Scotland, and Wales.

Brian L. Blakeley and Jacquelin Collins. *Documents in British History*. Vol. I: *Early Times to 1714.* 2nd ed. New York: McGraw-Hill, 1993. A valuable collection of historically significant documents, including the Magna Carta and eyewitness accounts of important battles and the Black Death.

John Cannon and Ralph Griffiths. *The Oxford Illustrated History of the British Monarchy.* 2nd ed. New York: Oxford University Press, 2001. A comprehensive and accessible look at the monarchy, including genealogical charts and photographs of royal residences and tombs.

Danny Danziger and John Gillingham. *1215: The Year of Magna Carta.* New York: Simon & Schuster, 2003. Danziger and Gillingham tackle the cultural aspects of the Middle Ages, including castles, churches, food, and politics leading up to the events at Runnymede and the signing of the Magna Carta.

Antonia Fraser, ed. *The Lives of the Kings & Queens of England.* Berkeley and Los Angeles: University of California Press, 1999. Noted British historians cover the royal houses of Britain and their monarchs. Sketches of the rulers' lives before they came to the throne are particularly valuable.

Plantagenet Somerset Fry. *Kings and Queens of England and Scotland.* New York: DK, 2011. A handy pocket reference of the British monarchy, with important highlights of each reign.

R.G. Grant, Ann Kay, Michael Kerrigan, and Philip Parker. *History of Britain and Ireland: The Definitive Visual Guide.* New York: DK, 2011. Richly illustrated guide to the monarchy and pivotal events that shaped the history of the British Isles.

Robert Lacey. *Great Tales from English History: A Treasury of True Stories About the Extraordinary People—Knights and Knaves, Rebels and Heroes, Queens and Commoners—Who Made Britain Great.* New York: Little, Brown, 2007. Lacey presents well-told anecdotes of British history that remind the reader that history is made by people and their various quirks and foibles.

Ian Mortimer. *The Time Traveler's Guide to Medieval England: A Handbook for Visitors to the Fourteenth Century.* New York: Touchstone/Simon & Schuster, 2008. A fascinating look at the life of everyday people in fourteenth-century England written in the style of a modern travel guide, covering the essentials of food, lodging, and how not to run afoul of the law.

Philip Wilkinson. *The British Monarchy for Dummies.* Chichester, UK: John Wiley and Sons, 2006. Wilkinson presents an accessible look at the monarchy, ensuring that readers remember that the rulers were people with human failings.

Periodicals and Internet Sources

Discovery News. "King Henry VIII's Madness Explained." History News, March 11, 2011. http://news.discovery.com/history/henry-viii-blood-disorder-110311.html.

Robert Hardman. "From the Unwelcome visitor at the Palace to the Joy of Losing Herself in a Crowd . . . Robert Hardman Reveals the Private Side of a Thoroughly Modern Monarch." *Daily Mail*, September 25, 2011. www.dailymail.co.uk/news/article-2041776/Queen-Elizabeth-Private-thoroughly-modern-monarch.html.

Robert Hardman. "'My Grandma Is Incredible,' Says Prince William in Exclusive, Unprecedented and Candid Interview with Author and Journalist Robert Hardman." *Daily Mail*, September 23, 2011. www.dailymail.co.uk/news/article-2041213/Prince-William-Queen-Elizabeth-exclusive-interview--My-grandma-incredible.html#ixzz1ZFwmFCqR.

Historic Royal Speeches and Writings: Edward VIII (r. Jan–December 1936). "Broadcast After His Abdication, 11 December 1936." www.royal.gov.uk/pdf/edwardviii.pdf.

Historic Royal Speeches and Writings: George VI (r. 1936–1952). www.royal.gov.uk/pdf/georgevi.pdf.

Historic Royal Speeches and Writings: Victoria (r. 1837–1901). http://www.royal.gov.uk/pdf/victoria.pdf.

Queen Elizabeth I. "Speech to the Troops at Tilbury." *Luminarium: Anthology of English Literature.* www.luminarium.org/renlit/tilbury.htm.

Science Daily. "Solving the Puzzle of Henry VII." Science News, March 3, 2011. www.sciencedaily.com/releases/2011/03/110303153114.htm.

Time. "The Royal Wedding." Features, May 16, 2011.

Websites

BBC—History (www.bbc.co.uk/history/). Covers a wide selection of topics. The "British History" section at www.bbc.co.uk/history/british/ provides summaries of important events in British history, such as the Magna Carta. The "Historic Figures" section at www.bbc.co.uk/history/historic_figures/ includes an alphabetized collection of biographical sketches of British monarchs and associated figures, such as Oliver Cromwell.

The London Gazette (www.london-gazette.co.uk/). The "Official Newspaper of Record" for Great Britain. Its archives contain almost 350 years of official proclamations, records of famous battles, and Parliamentary records.

The Middle Ages (www.middle-ages.org.uk). Contains several sections on important topics from 1066 to 1485, including studies of the Crusades, religion, weaponry, and monarchs.

The Official Website of the British Monarchy, "History of the Monarchy" (www.royal.gov.uk/Historyofthe Monarchy/HistoryoftheMonarchy .aspx). Covers the monarchs of England and Scotland, along with an archived video and image collection.

The Royal Channel: The Official Channel of the British Monarchy (www.you tube.com/user/TheRoyalChannel). The royals' YouTube channel contains videos of royal visits, official charities, and social welfare initiatives.

Wars of the Roses (www.warsofthe roses.com). Provides valuable information about the thirty-year upheaval and the competing claims to the English throne, including sketches of the important battles of the period.

Index

Howard, Catherine (wife of Henry VIII), 42, *43*
Hundred Years' War (1337–1453), 28, 31

I
India, 70, 90, 102
Indian Mutiny (Revolt of 1857), 90
Industrial Revolution, 76, 78, 79
Ireland, 59, 64, 97
Isabella (wife of Edward III), 26–27

J
James I (James VI of Scotland), 52, 53–56, *54*
James II, 61–62
John I (Lackland), 20–21
John of Gaunt (duke of Lancaster), 29

K
Katherine of Valois (wife of Henry V), 29, 31

L
Lackland, John. *See* John I
Lancaster, House of, 29–31
Leopold (king of Belgium), 84
Leopold V (duke of Austria), 19
Llywelyn (prince of Wales), 25–26
Long Parliament, 57–58, 63
Louis (prince of Battenburg), 96
Ludd, Ned, 78
Luddites, 78
Ludwig, George. *See* George I

M
MacDonald, Ramsey, 97
Magna Carta, 21, 22, 60
Major, John (historian), 35
Major, John (prime minister), 104, 107
Margaret (princess), 101, 104, 106
Margaret of Anjou (wife of Henry VI), 33, 34
Marlborough, Treaty of (1267), 23
Marshall, William (earl of Pembroke), 22
Mary, Queen of Scots, *48*, 48–49
Mary I (Bloody Mary), 46
Mary II, 62–64, *63*
Matilda (wife of Henry I), *15*, 16, 17–18

McLeod syndrome, 44
Melbourne, Lord, *83*, 84
Middleton, Catherine Elizabeth "Kate," 8–10, *9*, 106
Montgomery, Treaty of (1267), 25
Mortimer, Roger, 27
Mountbatten, Philip, 102

N
Neville, Richard (earl of Salisbury), 33, 35
Neville, Richard (earl of Warwick), 33, 34
Nicholas II (Russian czar), 92, *95*, 96
Northern Ireland, 97

O
Oates, Titus, 61
Odo of Bayeux, 14
Omdurman, Battle of (1898), 90–91, *91*
Ottoman Empire, 90

P
Paris, Treaty of (1259), 22
Paris, Treaty of (1763), 70
Paris, Treaty of (1783), 71–72
Parliament
    See also Long Parliament; Rump Parliament
    Henry III and, 23
    James I and, 53–54
Parr, Catherine (wife of Henry VIII), *43*, 43–44
Philip II (king of Spain), 50
Pius V (pope), 48
Plantagenet, Geoffrey, 16, 18
Plantagenet, House of, 23, 24, 29
    conflict between Lancaster and York branches of, 33
    ending of, 37
Plantagenet, Richard (duke of York), 31, 33
Popish Plot, 61
Protestant Reformation, 41
Puritanism, 57, 60

R
Raleigh, Walter, 49, 50
The Regency (1811—1820), 76
The Restoration, 60

Picture Credits

© Cover: North Wind / North Wind Picture Archives—All rights reserved.

© 19th era / Alamy, 15

© Agnew's, London, UK / The Bridgeman Art Library, 20

© Alfredo Dagli Orti / The Art Archive at Art Resource, NY, 68

© Apic / Hulton Archive / Getty Images, 72

© AP Images / Christine Nesbitt, 105

© AP Images / Dominic Lipinski, 9

© Archive Images / Alamy, 57

© The Art Archive at Art Resource, NY, 13

© Bettmann / Corbis, 101

© Classic Image / Alamy, 59

© Everett Collection, Inc. / Alamy, 7 (bottom), 27

© Gary Curtis / Alamy, 12

© HIP / Art Resource, NY, 6 (top), 63, 83

© Hulton Archive / Hulton Royals Collection / Getty Images, 7 (top), 55, 75, 103

© Lebrecht Music and Arts Photo Library / Alamy, 6 (bottom)

© Look and Learn / The Bridgeman Art Library, 22, 85

© Nathan Benn / Alamy, 47

© National Army Museum / The Art Archive at Art Resource, NY, 91

© National Trust Photo Library / Art Resource, NY, 77

© Niday Picture Library / Alamy, 86

© North Wind Picture Archives / Alamy, 54

© Popperfoto / Getty Images, 25, 95

© Portrait Essentials / Alamy, 43

© The Print Collector / Alamy, 36, 39, 89

© Réunion des Musées Nationaux / Art Resource, NY, 45

© The Stapleton Collection / The Bridgeman Art Library, 32

© Universal Images Group / Getty Images, 48, 51, 81, 99

© Visual Arts Library / Art Resource, NY, 30

About the Author

Andrew A. Kling's fascination with the British monarchy began as a youngster when his family spent a year in Cambridge, England. He discovered he was one of six Andrews in his classroom, all born the year after Prince Andrew. He was excused from school one day that year to see Queen Elizabeth II dedicate a memorial garden. He enjoys hockey and history, technology and trivia, books, movies, flags, and spending time with his wife and their famous Norwegian Forest cat, Chester.